INDIA'S SPACE ODYSSEY

From ancient skywatchers to modern-day space missions

INDIA'S

SPACE

ODYSSEY

From ancient skywatchers to modern-day space missions

DK Penguin Random House

Authors Nayan Keshan, Arushi Mathur
Illustrators Devika Awasthi, Priyal Mote
Editor Vatsal Verma
Project Art Editor Devika Awasthi
Art Editor Priyal Mote
Jacket designer Priyal Mote
DTP Designers Nand Kishor Acharya, Narender Kumar
Senior DTP Designer Tarun Sharma
Pre-Production Manager Sunil Sharma
Production Manager Pankaj Sharma
Picture Research Manager Taiyaba Khatoon
Managing Editor Chitra Subramanyam
Managing Art Editor Neha Ahuja Chowdhry
Senior Managing Art Editor Priyanka Thakur
Managing Director, India Aparna Sharma

First published in India in 2022 by
Dorling Kindersley Publishing Private Limited,
208, Ansal's Laxmi Deep
Laxmi Nagar District Centre
New Delhi 110092, India

10 9 8 7 6 5 4 3 2 1
001–326291–March/2022

A CIP catalogue record for this book is available from the British Library.

ISBN: 978-93-8837-297-8

Printed and bound in India

For the curious
www.dk.com

Contents

Looking up

Humans have always been fascinated by space. Cave paintings, created thousands of years ago, provide the earliest records of people looking at the stars. Later, astronomers began studying space by creating maps of the night sky. As technology developed, so did human dreams about space. However, actually going to space was still nothing more than a pipe dream.

STONE AGE GRAFFITI

It seems that after a long day of hunting and gathering, cave dwellers just wanted to unwind and let their inner artist loose. Sometimes, they looked up at the sky for inspiration. This cave painting in the Lascaux caves of southwestern France shows a cluster of six stars above a bull's shoulder, known as Pleiades.

UFO DREAMS

Fast forward a couple millennia and humans were already fantasizing about meeting aliens. Madhya Pradesh and Chhattisgarh in India have yielded some rock paintings that perhaps depict unidentified flying objects (UFOs) and odd-looking creatures with what appear to be helmets and antennae.

GREEK GEEKS

From 500 BCE to 200 CE, ancient Greek philosophers tried to answer some fundamental astronomical questions. While some answers were spot-on, others were a hit-and-miss. Heraclitus, for example, suggested that evaporations from the Earth's seas provide fuel for the stars, which burn like oil lamps.

CHINESE STARGAZERS

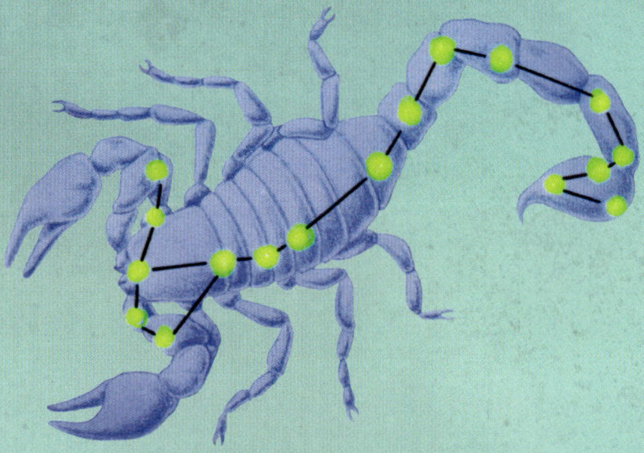

It is almost as if Chinese astronomers spent their entire lives looking up at the night sky – they recognized a total of 283 constellations. In around 700 CE, they drew up the Dunhuang Star Chart, which is the earliest-known map of the night sky.

THIS WAY OR THAT?

During the Age of Exploration (1450–1750 CE), oceans became the great frontier as people began to explore the Earth. Using scientific instruments, such as astrolabes and compasses, sailors measured the positions of heavenly bodies to navigate the seas. Star patterns helped them work out the directions.

A brass nautical compass

FAR-FETCHED FICTION

In the 19th century, writers such as Jules Verne and H G Wells paved the way for the science fiction genre. Verne's characters journeyed to the Moon in a shell fired by a giant cannon. Later, writers took inspiration from the *Star Trek* series. Bengali cartoonist Narayan Debnath's 1969 comic *Anjana Desh*, or In an Unknown Land, featured space explorers out to meet the inhabitants of other planets.

COMIC CAPERS

The dream of reaching space was at its peak in the comics of the mid-20th century. Belgian cartoonist Hergé's beloved characters, Tintin, Captain Haddock, and Snowy took a trip to the Moon in 1954. From their spacesuits to the rocket, everything was bafflingly accurate, even though it was way before the Apollo Moon Landing or the launch of the first satellite.

An embossed cover of Jules Verne's 1865 novel, *From the Earth to the Moon*

Eyes on the skies

Thousands of years ago, our ancestors were curious about regular phenomena such as the rising and setting of the Sun or the waning and waxing of the Moon. With time, they began formulating laws that govern these phenomena. Their observations were about how celestial bodies helped life on the Earth through religion.

A 19th-century painting of a Brahman astrologer

RELIGION AND SCIENCE

In ancient India, Brahmans served as priests, astronomers, and mathematicians. Stargazing and practising astrology also meant practising astronomy. Heavenly bodies represented divine entities and their worship was directed by religious texts, such as the Vedas.

TIMEKEEPING

As part astronomers, Brahmans created calendars. They divided the solar year into lunar months. They also developed the calculations for adding a leap month every five years so that the religious calendar corresponded with natural solar and lunar cycles. They also investigated constellations.

A Hindu calendar from Rajasthan, created in 1871–72

IMPORTANCE OF THE VEDAS

Vedic rites and rituals have a close connection with astronomical calculations and knowledge. The earliest formal Indian astronomical work is the *Vedanga Jyotisha*, which was mainly used to decide suitable times for performing sacrifices.

NAKSHATRAS

The ancient sages believed that the constellations, or *nakshatras*, helped override turbulences in human life. A myth about them relates that they were the 28 wives of the Moon god, Soma. He was cursed, because he favoured one of his wives, Rohini, which led to the waning and waxing cycle of the Moon.

An ivory carving, from 2nd–1st century, of the Moon god with his wife

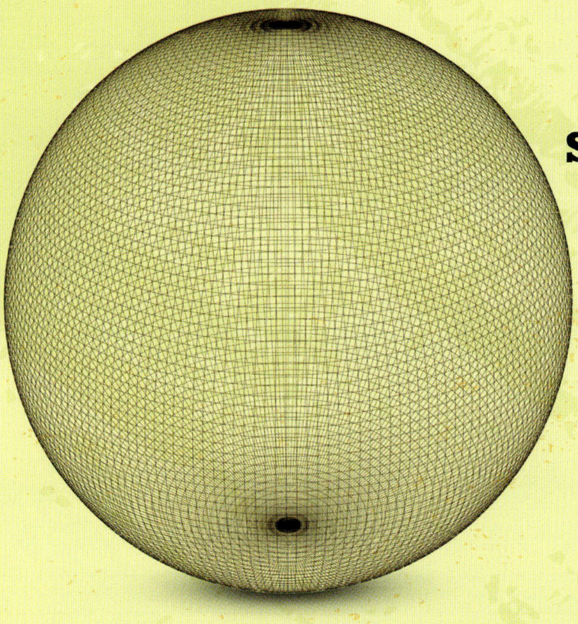

SIDDHANTIC ERA

This period saw the development of a new branch of astronomy, based on a series of books called the *Siddhantas*. By 1st century BCE, Indian astronomers proposed the similarity between the Sun and stars and that the Earth was spherical.

Panchanga

A manual and calendar, *panchanga* follows the traditional Hindu methods of timekeeping. It lists important religious events and their calculations in a tabulated manner. It also contains predictions about planetary positions, timings of sunrise and sunset, and other social, religious, and astrological information.

The scoop on space

The story of the birth of the universe is long and complex. It dates back to billions of years ago, when a violent explosion took place. It led to drastic changes in the composition and structure of the universe. In fact, the universe we live in today is a consequence of the processes that have taken place since then.

1

The universe was born from the Big Bang, an explosion that took place billions of years ago. It marked the start of time. Within a fraction of a second, the universe grew from being microscopically small to being thousands of light-years wide.

2

In the beginning, the young universe was immensely hot and dense. It was made of tiny radiation particles that produced tiny particles of matter. These combined to form the chemical elements, hydrogen and helium.

3

Hydrogen and helium nuclei combined with protons and electrons. The process resulted in the formation of atoms. These two elements produced all other elements that make up the universe today.

Scientists have found that it is possible to look at the universe's past by detecting cosmic microwave background radiation. It is the decaying heat energy of the Big Bang and is found everywhere.

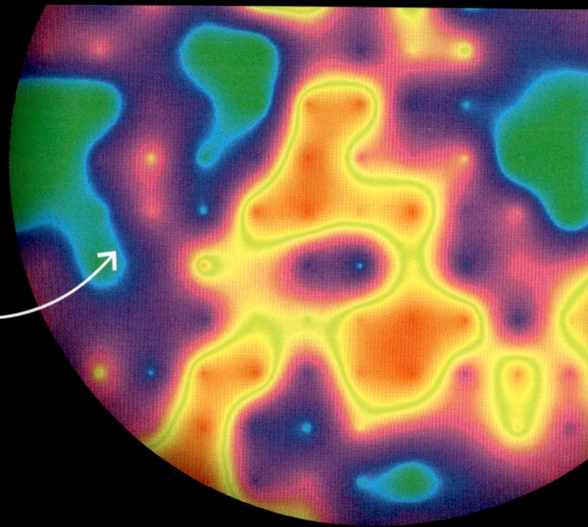

4

Some regions of the universe contained more hydrogen and helium than the others. In these places, the two gases and dark matter started to combine. It took millions of years for the first galaxies to appear. In these, the first stars were born.

5

The stars that appeared in the first galaxies had only hydrogen and helium. Soon, nuclear reactions began to take place in these stars. This resulted in the emission of other chemical elements that found their way into space as these stars disintegrated.

6

Over time, different galaxies interacted with each other. Some merged to form bigger galaxies, each with multiple solar systems.

Ancient skywatchers

Astronomical science took many twists and turns spanning centuries before finally deciphering the actual order of the solar system and the universe. Many ancient astronomers, scientists, and mathematicians played an important role in this.

ARISTOTLE

Considered one of the greatest thinkers to have ever lived, Greek philosopher and scientist Aristotle believed that the Earth was round and at the centre of the universe. According to him, all other celestial bodies, such as the Sun and the planets, moved around it in concentric circles. His ideas were later discounted.

PTOLEMY

Fascinated by the sky, Egyptian philosopher and scientist Ptolemy listed 1,022 stars and 48 constellations. The list is still used today. He supported Aristotle's theory as well.

ARYABHATA

Indian mathematician and astronomer Aryabhata suggested that stars and heavenly bodies were all stationary, but appeared moving as the Earth was rotating. Unfortunately, nobody believed his theory at that time.

VARAHAMIHIRA

Indian philosopher, astronomer, and mathematician Varahamihira, also known as Varaha or Mihira, proposed that the Moon does not have any light of its own. The Moon and the other planets, he believed, were lustrous as they reflected the Sun's light.

BRAHMAGUPTA

An eminent Indian mathematician and astronomer in his time, Brahmagupta argued against Aryabhata's theory. He claimed that the Earth is static and the heavenly bodies moved around it. He also identified the Earth's gravitational force and noted that the Earth naturally attracted all bodies towards itself.

COPERNICUS

The theories of Polish astronomer Nicolaus Copernicus revolutionized the way humans understood space and its elements. He laid the foundations for future astronomers by correctly establishing the idea that the Sun was at the centre of the universe and the planets, including the Earth, revolved around it.

GALILEO

He was the first person to use a telescope to explore the night sky. An Italian philosopher, astronomer, and mathematician, Galileo Galilei found clues that proved the Earth revolved around the Sun. Because his findings contradicted the Catholic Church's teachings, he was punished and placed under house arrest.

Elements of space

Space consists of different types of objects. Some of these can actually be seen, but there are many that are difficult to detect. Together, they make up our beautiful universe.

UNIVERSE
Space and everything in it – from stars and galaxies to every living being on the Earth – is the universe. It started with an explosion called the Big Bang and has been expanding ever since.

Fun fact

Space begins about 100 km (60 miles) above the Earth's surface.

NEBULAE
Gigantic clouds of gas and dust called nebulae exist in the vast expanses of space between stars. While some are the birthplaces for stars, others form as stars die.

Did you know?

The universe was formed in a fraction of a second and started out smaller than a single atom.

GALAXIES

Giant star groups are called galaxies. There are billions of galaxies in the universe, each comprising billions of stars which rotate around its centre. Galaxies come in different sizes and shapes.

MILKY WAY

Our solar system is a part of a spiral galaxy called the Milky Way. It consists of billions of stars, including the Sun. From the Earth, the Milky Way looks like a thick starry band stretching across the sky. It takes 100,000 light years to travel from edge to edge.

SOLAR SYSTEM

The eight planets that revolve around our closest star, the Sun, make up the solar system. It also consists of other celestial bodies, such as moons, comets, and asteroids.

SUN

At the centre of our solar system lies a fiery ball of gas called the Sun. It is not different from other stars in space, but looks enormous because of its proximity to the Earth. The planets travel around it in oval-shaped paths called orbits.

We are here

The Earth may seem huge to us, but it is just one tiny speck in space. The universe is too large to comprehend. This is how we fit into the scale of the universe.

Made up of at least 200 billion galaxies, spanning at least 156 light years, the universe is always expanding and may not even have an outer edge.

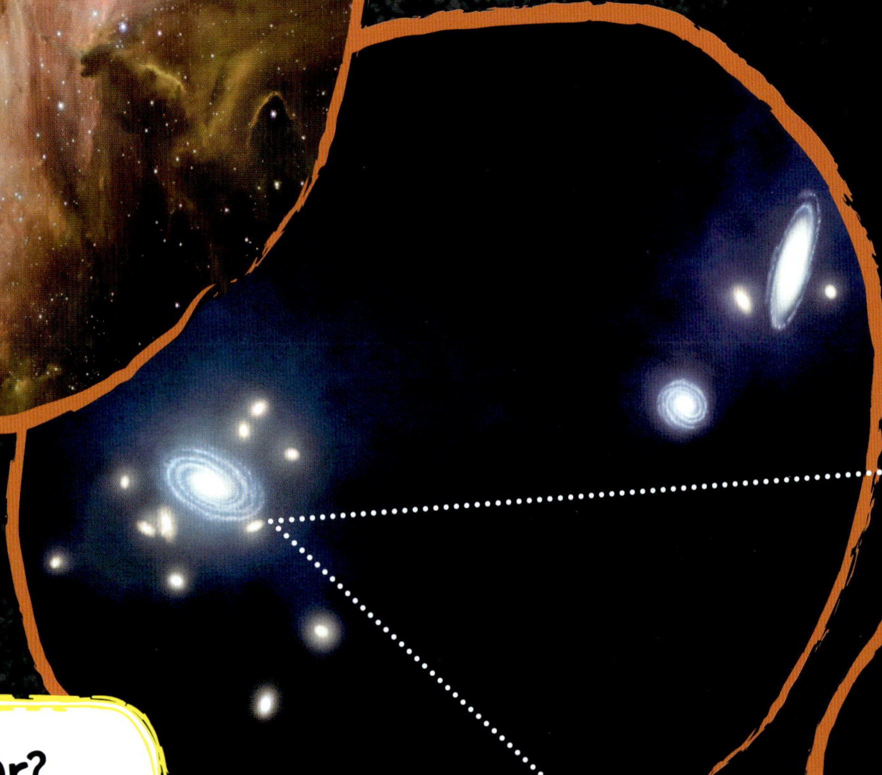

What is a light year?

Distances in space are measured in a unit called light year. It is the distance that light, which is the fastest thing in the universe, travels in one year. One light year is about 9.5 trillion km (5.9 trillion miles).

Our home galaxy, the Milky Way, is part of a galaxy group called the Local Group. The cluster is about 10 million light years across and the Milky Way is one of the bigger galaxies in the group.

We live here – in cities, towns, and villages on the Earth. But, humans can not even be seen with the naked eye when viewed from outer space. Now, imagine your place in the entire cosmic scheme of things.

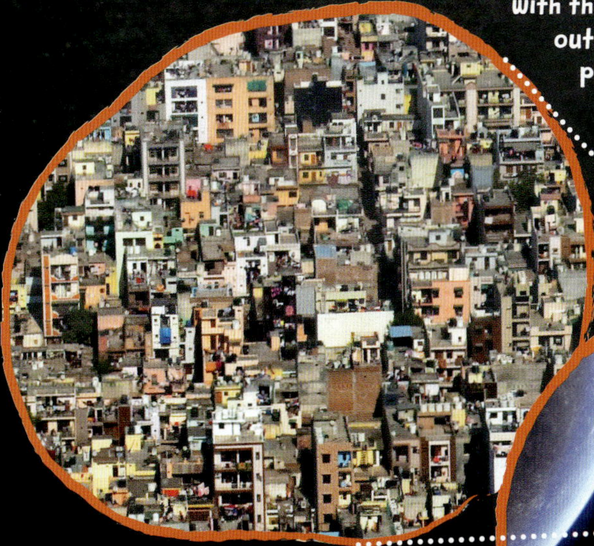

The Earth is part of our solar system. About 12,742 km (7,918 miles) across, it is the only planet known to support human life. It has one natural satellite – the Moon.

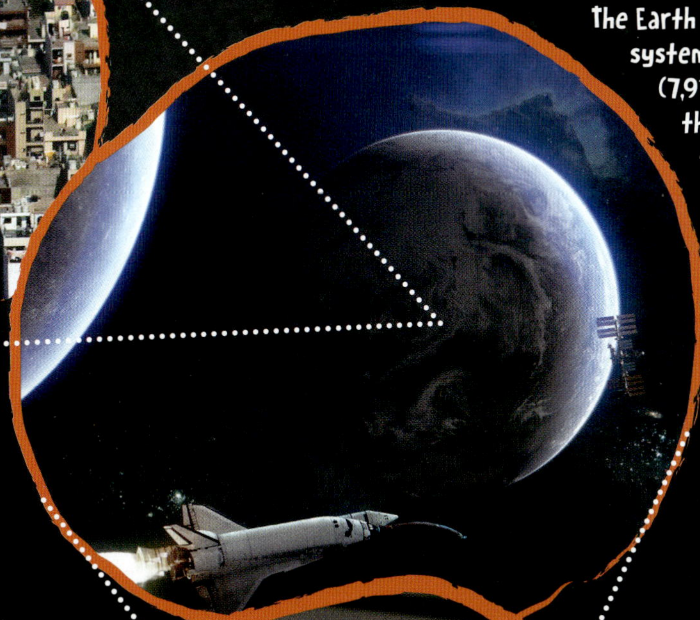

On the edge of one of the spiral arms of the Milky Way sits our solar system. It includes planets, their moons, comets, asteroids, meteoroids, dust, and gas.

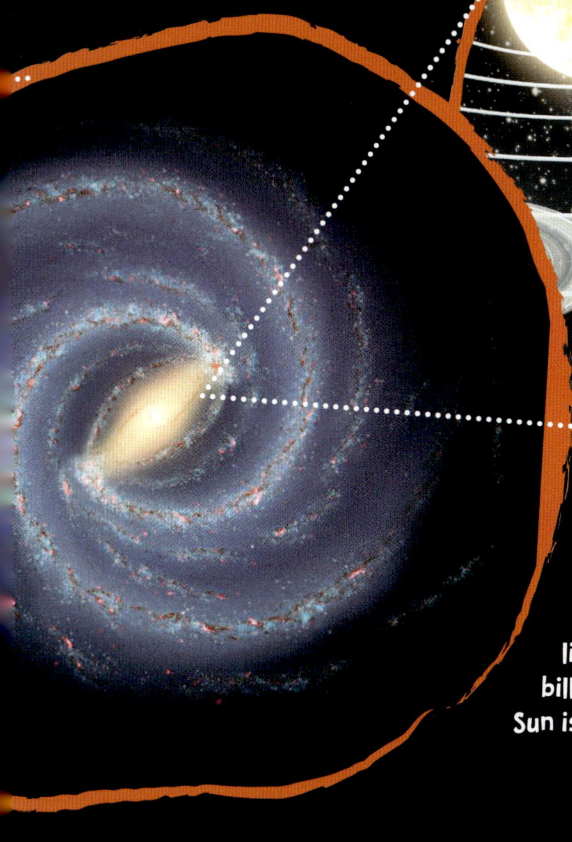

A spiral galaxy, with arms emanating from its centre, the Milky Way is 100,000 light years across. It has billions of stars and our Sun is just one of them.

The solar system

Scientists believe that the solar system began to form around 4.6 billion years ago. The Sun appeared first as clouds of dust and gas came together. Soon, the planets and other objects began to orbit it due to its gravity.

THE PLANETS

The eight planets are classified into three categories. Rocky planets – Mercury, Venus, Earth, and Mars – are small and have solid surfaces. Gas giants – Jupiter and Saturn – are huge balls of gas. Ice giants – Uranus and Neptune – are made of gas and icy material.

SUN

A middle-aged star, the Sun mainly comprises hydrogen and helium. It is the primary source of heat and light for life on the Earth. All planets travel around it because of its gravitational pull.

MERCURY

It is the smallest of the eight planets and nearest to the Sun. It takes only 88 days to orbit around the Sun.

VENUS

The warmest planet of the solar system, Venus has a thick and dense atmosphere.

EARTH

Our home, the Earth, is the only known planet to support life. Unlike other planets, it is neither too hot nor too cold.

MARS

Known as the Red Planet, it has a rocky surface, polar ice caps, mountains, valleys, and clouds.

ASTEROID BELT

Between the orbits of Mars and Jupiter lies a ring of big rocks, called asteroids.

JUPITER

The biggest planet in our solar system, Jupiter has the most number of moons.

Kuiper belt

Beyond Neptune's orbit lies a band of millions of frozen objects. Called the Kuiper Belt, it is home to dwarf planets, such as Pluto, Haumea, Eris, and Makemake, and comets, which are lumps of rock and ice. Sometimes, icy chunks from this region come closer to the Sun, heat up, and produce bright tails.

An artist's impression of Kuiper Belt objects

Milky Way's centre

The heart of the Milky Way galaxy, known as the Galactic Centre, is shrouded in floating clouds of dust and gas, making it difficult for optical telescopes to reveal its mysteries. Scientists have to use infrared radiation to study it. In this infrared image from the Spitzer Space Telescope, one can see the Galactic Centre as a bright central spot, with the galactic plane crowded with clouds and stars. The Galactic Centre is possibly home to a supermassive black hole, millions of times bigger than the Sun. Hundreds of thousands of stars whirl around it at a torrential speed.

Aryabhata

Born in 476 CE, possibly in the Gupta captial of Kusumapura, corresponding to present-day Patna in the state of Bihar, Aryabhata redefined the concept of zero by giving it a value. Even though many of his astronomical ideas were not accepted right away, he revolutionized the understanding of the Earth's behaviour. This is an imagined conversation with him.

Q. Could you please tell us a little about the books you have written?

A. I have written two books, the *Aryabhatiya* and the *Aryabhatasiddhanta*. These contain my thoughts on mathematics and astronomy, two of my favourite subjects. I wrote the *Aryabhatasiddhanta* so long ago that all copies of that work are lost. But from what I can remember, it was extremely popular in northwestern India and among the people of the Sasanian Dynasty of Iran. In fact, the Sasanians liked it so much that they used it in Islamic astronomy. My contemporaries and later some Indian astronomers, such as Varahamihira, Bhaskara I, and Brahmagupta, preserved some of *Aryabhatasiddhanta*'s contents. But I don't know what became of the text after that.

Q. What about the *Aryabhatiya* though?

A. It was published in 499 CE. I divided it into three sections – "Ganita", or mathematics, "Kala-kriya", or time calculations, and "Gola", or sphere. For the purpose of this interview, let me focus more on the astronomy part of the text and talk about the second and the third sections. "Kala-kriya" mainly talks about planetary motion along the ecliptic, which is the »

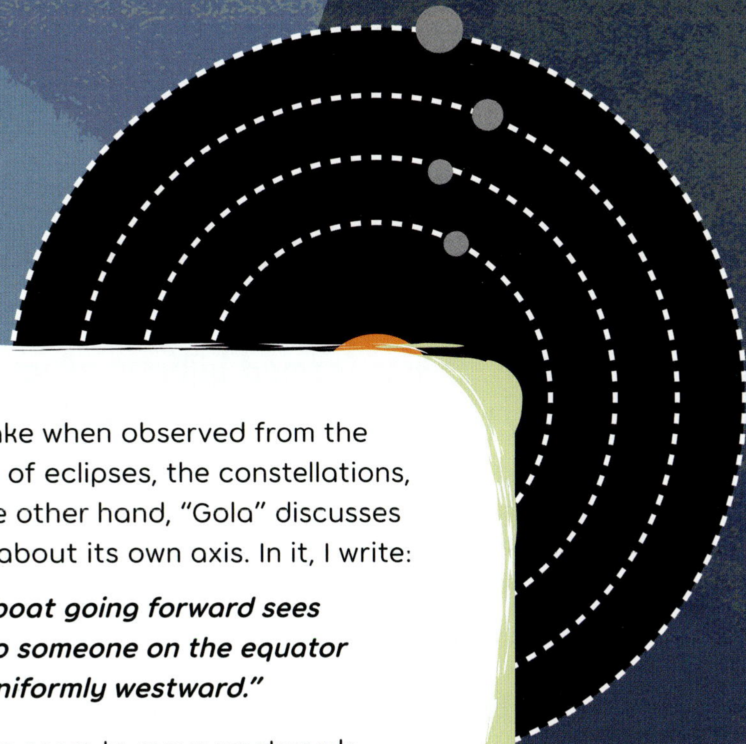

» apparent path that the Sun seems to take when observed from the Earth. We can use it to pinpoint the location of eclipses, the constellations, the Moon, and neighbouring planets. On the other hand, "Gola" discusses the Earth's spherical shape and its rotation about its own axis. In it, I write:

"In the same way that someone in a boat going forward sees an unmoving object going backward, so someone on the equator sees the unmoving stars going uniformly westward."

This means that to us, on Earth, the stars seem to move westwards across the sky. But, this is an illusion. It is we who are moving and not the stars. The Earth's rotation makes all other celestial bodies appear to be in motion.

Q. We have heard that some of the things you mentioned in "Gola" were controversial during that time?

A. People take time to grasp and accept new ideas. I think that I was just a little ahead of my time. No one believed me when I wrote about the Earth spinning on its axis. It was only when Polish astronomer Nicolaus Copernicus endorsed my idea that people started to take it seriously. Even then, it wasn't until the mid-17th century that this notion was widely accepted.

Q. It is good to know that your ideas were finally accepted. Tell us about your other findings.

A. I also calculated the length of the sidereal day and the sidereal year. While the sidereal day is the time that the Earth takes to rotate once in relation to the stars, the sidereal year is the time it takes to complete one revolution in its orbit in relation to the stars. Both of these calculations were almost faultless.

The Earth

Called the "blue planet" or the "blue marble", the Earth is home to a large number of people, plants, and animals. It was formed billions of years ago when clouds of rock, dust, and gas came together to form a molten sphere, part of which eventually solidified.

THRIVING LIFE

The Earth is the only known body in the universe to support life. This is because it has all the right conditions. So, it is at just the right distance from the Sun, making the planet neither too hot nor too cold. It has liquid water and other raw materials, such as soil. It is also surrounded by a thick gaseous blanket that protects us from hazardous elements of outer space.

Did you know?

No one has drilled deep enough to reach the Earth's centre. Scientists have made observations about the Earth's layers by studying vibrations during earthquakes.

This image of the Earth was taken from the *Apollo 11* spacecraft.

EARTHRISE

Just as you would see a moonrise or sunrise from the Earth, you would also see the Earth rising over the Moon's horizon. However, unlike the Moon and the Sun that appear to move across the sky, the Earth appears stationary.

Northern lights at Kirkjufell mountain in Iceland.

LIGHT FANTASTIC

When tiny solar particles collide with molecules of oxygen and nitrogen in the Earth's atmosphere, the electrons in the molecules emit colourful lights. This dazzling natural light show is called aurora borealis, or northern lights, in the North Pole and aurora australis, or southern lights, in the South Pole.

INSIDE THE EARTH

If you cut the Earth in half, you would see that it is made up of several layers. Its outer layer, called the crust, is solid and rocky. Its middle layer is called the mantle. While the lower mantle is solid rock, the upper mantle can move like a liquid. The deepest part of the Earth is called the core. It has two sections – the outer layer of liquid metals and the inner ball of solid metal.

The Sun

Shining bright in the sky during the day, the Sun is a huge ball of hot gases held together by gravity. The largest object in the solar system, it acts as its fulcrum and plays a crucial role in supporting life on the Earth.

Did you know?

At the Sun's core, temperatures can go upto 29 million°F (16 million°C).

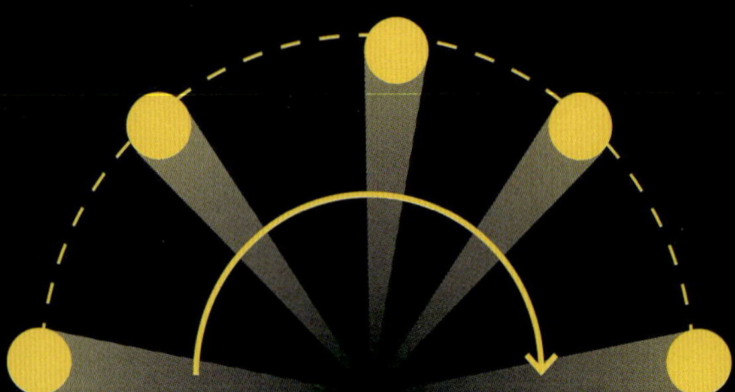

MOVING SUN

It may seem to us on the Earth that the Sun is moving across the sky each day. But, in reality, the Sun is stationary. It is the Earth that spins on its axis and its rotation causes the illusion of the Sun's movement.

SOLAR ECLIPSE

Sometimes, the Moon passes between the Earth and the Sun, blocking the sunlight to reach certain parts of the Earth. This event is called a solar eclipse. When the Moon covers only a part of the Sun, it is called a partial solar eclipse. During a total solar eclipse, the Sun appears as a faintly glowing ring.

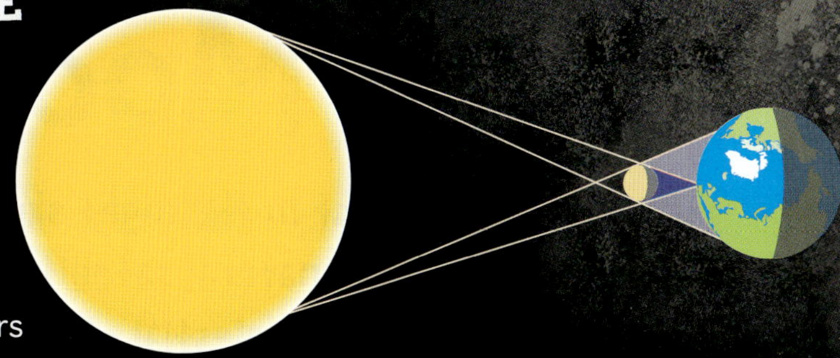

Energy from the core moves up through the two inner layers – the radiative zone and the convective zone – before reaching the surface.

The Sun's fiery surface is called the photosphere.

In 2018, NASA launched the Parker Solar Probe to study the Sun. Three years later, the probe flew through the outer atmosphere of the Sun – the first for any spacecraft. In its flyby, it explored the solar particles and the magnetic fields. Scientists anticipate that this major breakthrough will help them unravel many mysteries of the Sun.

WHAT LIES AHEAD

Like every other star in the Space, the Sun will also eventually perish. Scientists estimate that it was born around 4.6 billion years ago and in another 5 billion years, it will exhaust its supply of hydrogen. It will then kick-start the helium-burning process and swell to many times its size before collapsing.

The Moon

The brightest object in the night sky, the Moon is the Earth's only natural satellite. Till date, it remains the only celestial object that has witnessed human visits.

STRUCTURE AND COMPOSITION

The Moon's outer layer, or crust, is made of calcium-rich rocks. Below the crust is the mantle, thought to be rich in minerals. The mantle may be partially molten in the deeper areas. At the centre, it may have a small metal core.

MASSIVE COLLISION

Scientists believe that the Moon was formed as a result of a collision between a large asteroid and the Earth. The debris from the two bodies started to orbit the Earth and later combined to form the Moon.

Fun Fact

If you stretch the Moon's surface out so that it is flat, it would only cover North and South America.

LUNAR TIDES

The Moon's gravitational pull causes ocean waters on the Earth to rise and fall. While low tides occur when a place is at right angles to the Moon's gravity pull, high tides occur when a place is aligned with the Moon.

MISSIONS

In 1959, the USSR launched *Luna 2* – the first probe to reach the Moon's surface. A few weeks later, *Luna 3* beamed back the first photos of the far side of the Moon. It was during NASA's *Apollo 11* mission, launched in 1969, that humans first set foot on the Moon. In 2008, ISRO launched *Chandrayaan-1*, which was instrumental in the discovery of water ice on the Moon.

NASA staff working on the *Lunar Prospector* orbiter

MOON'S SURFACE

The surface of the Moon is full of craters, which are roughly circular depressions. This is because several meteors and asteroids have hit it over time.

A map in the sky

Throughout history, seafarers have relied upon celestial bodies for navigational guidance. Initially, sailors used the coastline as a guide. But later, they discovered that stars could be efficient navigational tools. Today, space agencies have developed sophisticated techniques to navigate missions outside the Earth's atmosphere using celestial bodies.

IT'S CALLED WAYFINDING

The Polynesian navigators forged paths across the Pacific Ocean by carefully noting the ocean swell and the position of the celestial bodies. They used stick charts, made from natural materials, to record wave patterns. The Vikings used simple sundials to work out the elevation of the Sun in order to sail along a line of latitude. By calculating the height of the Sun or certain stars, the ancient Greeks, too, were able to determine their latitude.

MOTION OF STARS

The early sailors needed a constant reference point to mark their geographical positions. Thus, stars and their patterns came in handy as navigational tools. For example, people searched for the Big Dipper to identify the north sky and the Pole Star to determine the north-south direction in the northern hemisphere.

Magnetic compass

GOODBYE DEAD RECKONING

For sailors, celestial navigation was a step ahead from dead reckoning, which relied on the celestial bodies and the horizon to calculate a vessel's position. When the Chinese invented the magnetic compass, it was a major breakthrough as it meant that sailors could orient themselves and find their way even at night or when visibility was low.

THE PRECISE WAY FORWARD

By understanding the statistics of the sky, seafarers were able to create a system of longitude and latitude to find their exact location and create reliable maps. While latitude was easy to determine, a "universal clock" was required for longitude. The invention of the chronometer in the 18th century was the answer to this age-old problem.

An 18th-century chronometer

Endurance Expedition

While Irish explorer Ernest Shackleton was crossing Antarctica, his ship *Endurance* was crushed by thick ice in the Weddell Sea. Shackleton and five crew members sailed through stormy seas, armed with a sextant, to the nearest inhabited place. Any mistake with the navigation would have cost them their life as there was no land downwind for more than 12,500 km (7,767 miles).

A 1987 Hungarian stamp showing Shackleton and emperor penguins, which are endemic to Antarctica

Instruments

In the beginning, people observed the skies with just their eyes. Over the years, as human curiosity about space grew, scientists devised different tools for space observation.

TELESCOPE

This instrument allows people to gaze at celestial bodies far away. It was invented in 1608 by Dutch lens maker Hans Lippershey. But it was Italian physicist Galileo who first used it to observe the sky.

CHRONOMETER

In 1730, English horologist John Harrison invented a special clock to keep time at sea. Called chronometer, it also helped sailors to know their exact location by determining the longitude.

ASTROLABE

Travellers used an astrolabe to tell how far north or south they were, as it showed them their latitude on the Earth. The Greeks were the first to use an astrolabe but it was improved by Arabs, who added more dials and discs to make it more accurate.

CROSS-STAFF

From the late 15th century onwards, navigators used the cross-staff to determine the latitude of their ships. This instrument gave them the Sun's height above the horizon. They used this measurement to calculate the latitude.

COMPASS

Invented in China around 2,000 years ago, its needle always points towards the North Pole. This made it a handy instrument for sailors to find their way.

OCTANT AND SEXTANT

An octant enabled the sailors to measure the altitude of the Sun, the Moon, or stars in order to find their latitude. Its accuracy was further improved to develop the sextant. While octants were mostly made of wood and ivory, sextants were made of brass.

Sundial

Since ancient times, people have been using sundials to calculate time. This device uses shadows cast by the Sun to show the time of day.

BUILD YOUR OWN SUNDIAL

With just a few things from your stationery stash, you can build your own sundial. Ask an adult for help to cut the wood.

GNOMON

The part of the sundial that casts a shadow is called a gnomon. It is important that the gnomon lines up with the Earth's axis. For this, set the gnomon at an angle equal to your latitude. You can use an atlas to know your latitude.

STEP 1

Draw a straight line across a wooden board and then draw lines 15° apart from its central point. Write the times as shown on the right.

STEP 2

With help of an adult, cut a piece of wood into a triangle such that one of its angles is equal to that of your latitude.

STEP 3

Use clay to fix a pencil on the central point and stick the wooden triangle under it. Take the sundial outside and observe the shadow cast by the gnomon.

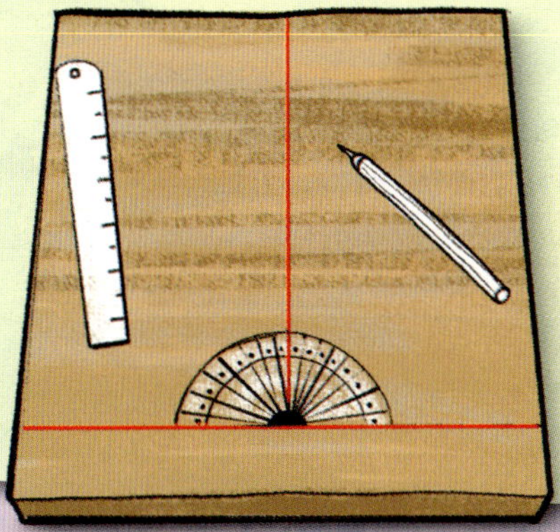

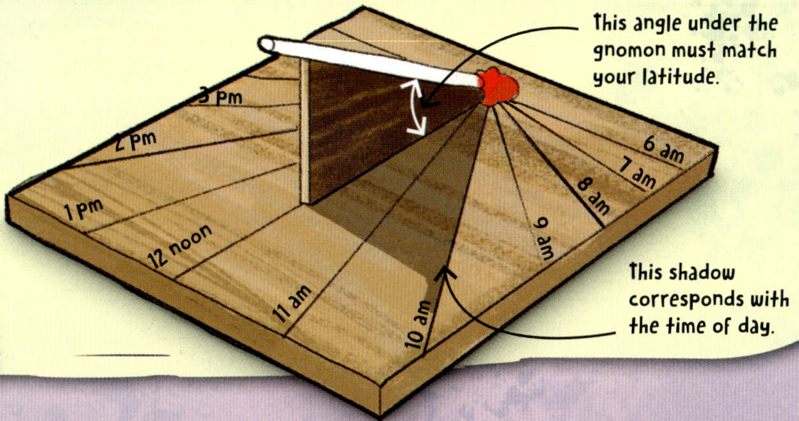

Solar worship

Thousands of years before anyone had even thought about a telescope or a spacecraft, our ancestors gazed up at the night sky with fascination, reverence, and a deep desire to know more. As a way of understanding their relationship with the universe, they introduced celestial bodies, such as the Sun, into folklore and mythology.

SURYA

The Sun god in Hinduism, Surya is worshipped as the creator of the universe and the source of all life. Each day, he is believed to travel across the sky in his golden chariot pulled by seven horses and driven by Aruna, the personification of dawn.

HELIOS AND APOLLO

In Greek mythology, the Sun god is called Helios. Like Surya, he also drives his chariot across the sky each day. He is associated with Apollo, who is said to have brought light to the Earth.

RA

Ancient Egyptians believed that their Sun god, Ra, sailed through the heavens in his barque to bring the Sun to the land. They also believed that every night, the sky goddess Nut swallowed Ra who was then reborn the following morning.

Myths around the Sun

There are many mythological stories surrounding the Sun. In some cultures, the Sun disappears, depriving the world of food and warmth. In others, it is looked at as the father of the universe, whose rising and setting symbolizes birth, death, and resurrection.

AMATERASU

A popular story in Japan's Shinto religion tells of how the Sun goddess, Amaterasu, once took offence at her brother's jest and hid in a cave. The world was temporarily deprived of the Sun. The other gods had to lure her out for light to be restored to the world once again.

SHAMASH

Babylonians believed that each morning, the Sun god, Shamash, travelled from his home in the Mountain of the East across the sky to the Mountain of the West. The Sumerians saw the solar rays as heavenly judgements, sent to strike humankind.

INTI

The Sun god of the Incas of South America, Inti was worshipped not only for providing warmth, but also for bringing rain. He was seen as the father of the Inca emperors.

Lunar worship

As the brightest heavenly body visible in the night sky, the Moon has an incredible influence on our lives. Our ancestors observed it and wondered about it just as we do today. In many cultures, the gods and goddesses of the Moon are among the most important deities.

CHANDRA

In Hinduism, there are multiple legends about Chandra, the Moon god, who rode across the sky in a chariot drawn by 10 white horses. He is also associated with Soma, the healing elixir that grants immortality.

CHANG'E

One of the most popular deities in ancient China was Chang'e, the goddess of the Moon. A legend describes how she became immortal after consuming the elixir of immortality and flew to the Moon. From then on, she came to be worshipped as a lunar deity.

LUNA AND SELENE

In ancient Rome, the goddess Luna was often pictured with a crescent Moon on her head. She was known as the bringer of light. In Greek mythology, Selene is the goddess of the Moon, who drove her chariot across the celestial realm.

TARQEQ

The Inuits of Alaska believed in the spirit of the Moon, Tarqeq, a great hunter who watched over the behaviour of humans from the sky.

THOTH

An ancient Egyptian Moon god, Thoth was usually depicted as a man with the head of an ibis, a water bird. The Egyptians believed that he invented writing and made calculations to form the heavens, and ran the calendar. Later, ancient Greeks credited him with inventing astronomy and other sciences.

NANNA AND SIN

One of the earliest records of Moon worship is found in the ancient civilization of Mesopotamia. In its city of Ur, people built a giant temple where they worshipped their Moon god, Nanna. Some 1,500 years later, people of a new civilization, called Babylonia, used it to honour their own Moon god, Sin.

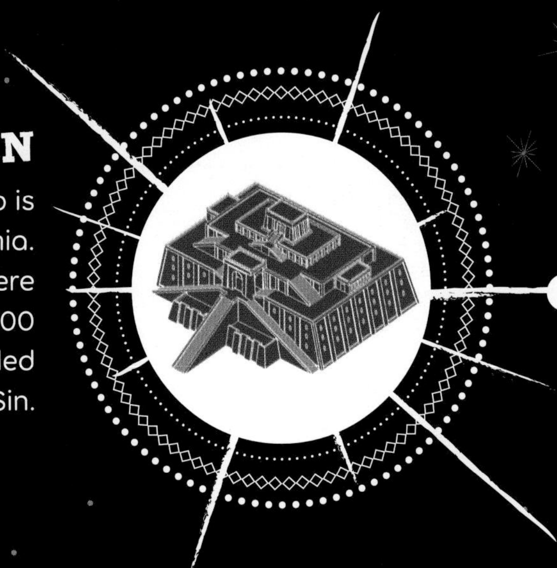

ANIMAL SHAPESHIFTERS

The myth of some humans transforming into bloodthirsty wolves on full Moon nights was highly popular in medieval Europe, where the wolf was the most feared wild animal. Elsewhere, animal shapeshifters included jaguars, tigers, and foxes.

Immortals in the night sky

The awe-inspiring mysteries of the universe and the unknown of space have held sway over humans for thousands of years. Everything in it, including its origin, shape, and order, is thought to have a deeper meaning. Stars and planets, like beacons in the night sky, are believed to influence human life, often as divine beings.

NAVAGRAHA

In Hinduism, Navagraha is a collection of nine celestial bodies, which are seen as deities and believed to influence human fate on the Earth. Each *graha*, or planet, is associated with one quality. For instance, worship of the fiery Mangala leads to freedom from poverty and illness.

Bronze statue of Jupiter from 1st–2nd century

ROMAN GODS

The ancient Romans named the five planets they could see with their naked eye after their gods. We still use the same names for Mercury, Venus, Mars, Jupiter, and Saturn. Uranus and Neptune were discovered later but they, too, were named after Roman gods. The planets and the gods were given similar characteristics. For example, Mars was named after the god of war, possibly from the fact that the planet is red, much like blood.

CONSTELLATIONS

Ancient Greeks believed that constellations were placed in the sky by their gods to serve as lessons. They were named after characters from mythology. For example, the constellation Centaurus was named after centaur – a mythical creature that is half horse, half human.

The Hindu epic *Mahabharata* along with other Hindu religious texts mentions the constellation Ursa Major, or the Big Dipper, as Saptarishi Mandal representing seven powerful and divine sages that reside together in the sky.

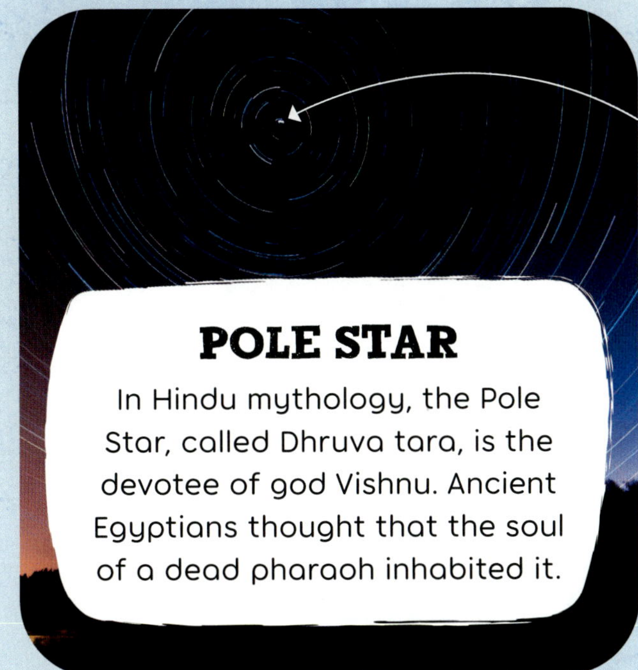

Pole Star in the night sky

POLE STAR

In Hindu mythology, the Pole Star, called Dhruva tara, is the devotee of god Vishnu. Ancient Egyptians thought that the soul of a dead pharaoh inhabited it.

MILKY WAY

The Aztecs and the Mayans referred to the Milky Way as a white serpent writhing across the night sky. Some other cultures believed that it was a road or a river linking the Earth and the Heaven. While for Indigenous Americans, it was a pathway to the land of the dead, the Inca imagined it as a heavenly river.

STARS

In many cultures, stars are also deified. The Mesopotamian goddess Ishtar is often portrayed as an eight-pointed star. The Egyptian goddess Isis is equated with the star Sirius.

Sirius in its constellation Canis Major or the Greater Dog

Did you know?

In 1930, an 11-year-old girl, Venetia Burney, suggested the name Pluto for the planet, after the god of underworld, as she thought that it was ideal for a dark, cold planet.

Vedanga Jyotisha

One of the earliest known texts on Indian astronomy, *Vedanga Jyotisha* is proof that interest in astronomy has existed in India since ancient times. A sacred text, it laid the foundations of Jyotisha, which is the traditional Hindu system of astrology. It was also the first to list the *nakshatras*.

Part of the Vedas, the *Vedanga Jyotisha* is estimated to have been composed between the 12th and 14th centuries BCE by sage Lagadha. This Sanskrit text is presented in two editions, with only some minor differences between them.

The Rigvedic edition of the *Vedanga Jyotisha* includes **36** verses.

The Yajurvedic edition of the *Vedanga Jyotisha* includes **43** verses.

The *Vedanga Jyotisha* is a manual that records the fundamentals of astronomy, which were essential for everyday life of people in the Vedic Age. For example, the text describes the main movements of the Sun and the Moon. It also gives mathematical formulae to determine a particular time during the day or night, the day of the week or the fortnight, the duration of seasons, and the month and the year. So people referred to it to make calendars and astrological charts.

Many Hindus believe that knowledge of the movements of the heavenly bodies and celestial phenomena, such as eclipses and solstices, is necessary for social and religious life. For this purpose, the *Vedanga Jyotisha* was a handy text during Vedic times. People relied on it to determine auspicious moments for rituals, ceremonies, and festivities. They also consulted it to know the influence of each heavenly object on their lives and the events of the world.

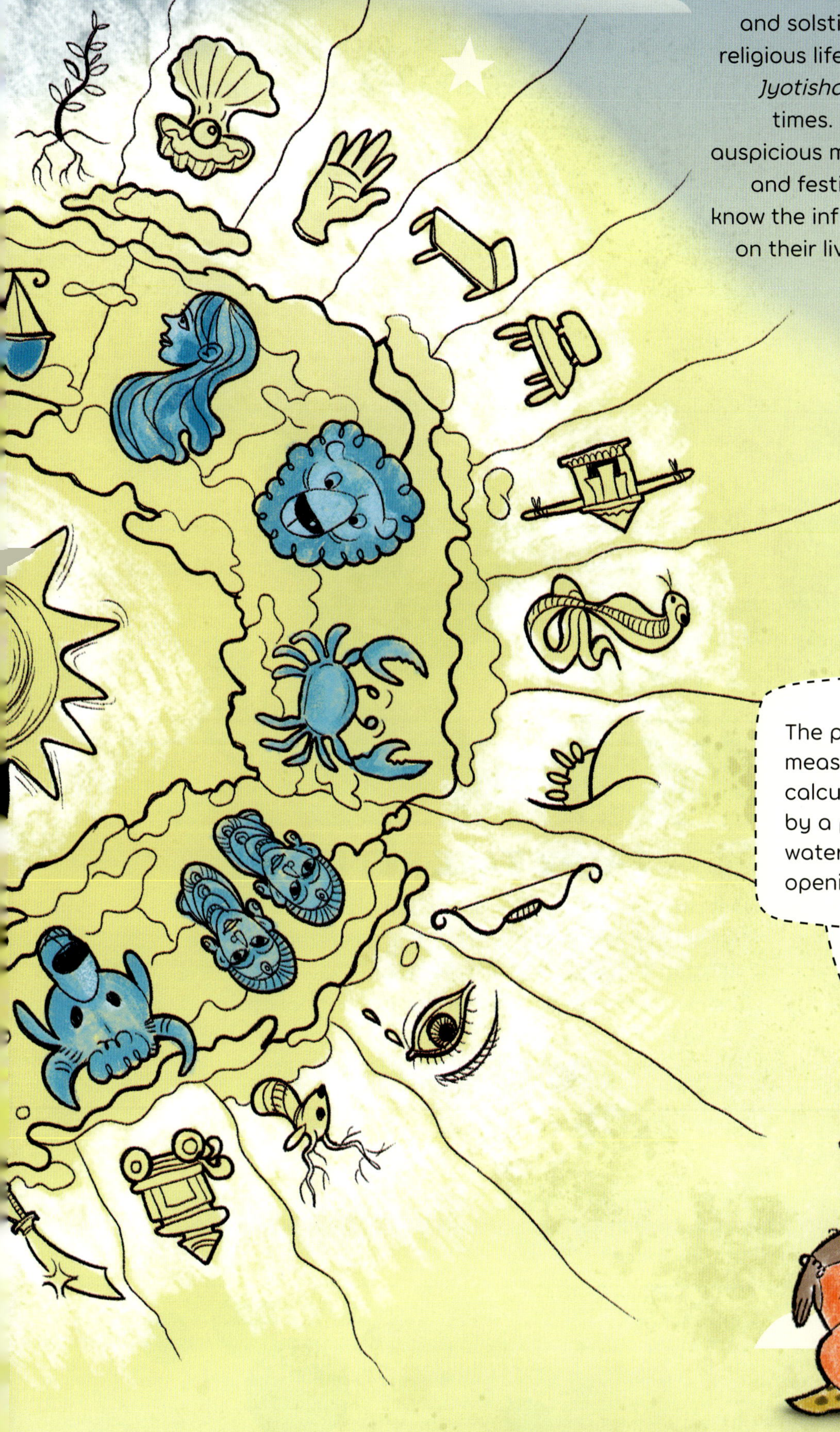

A Jyotisha chart showing zodiac signs in inner circle and their corresponding *nakshatras* in outer circle

Is anybody out there?

There are more than a billion galaxies in the universe. Each galaxy has billions of stars and every star may have its own solar system. Just thinking about the number of planets and moons in the universe is enough to make anyone's head spin. It is reasonable to believe that apart from the Earth, there may be life elsewhere in the cosmos.

Artist's impression of surface of a planet outside our solar system

FAIRY TALE SETTING

Astronomers search for Earth-like planets by locating them in the Goldilocks zone. It is a reference to the fairy tale in which a girl called Goldilocks prefers the bowl of porridge that is neither too hot nor too cold. A Goldilocks planet will have to be neither too close nor too far from its sun to sustain life.

RECIPE FOR LIFE

All life forms that we know of are made up of cells. The cells consist of chemical elements, which are found in abundance throughout the universe. So it would be rather strange for life to not have developed elsewhere.

Fun fact

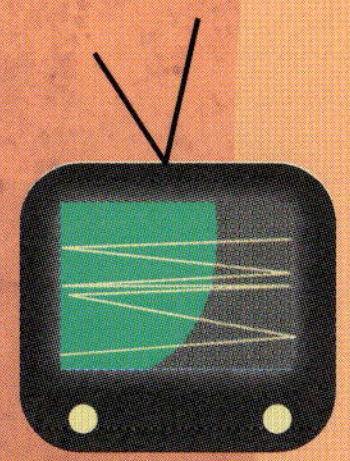

The very first television signals, transmitted in 1932, have already travelled more than 75 light years. These could potentially be the first signals from the Earth that an extraterrestrial might receive.

SIGNALS FROM SKY

An organization called Search for Extraterrestrial Intelligence (SETI) uses powerful radio telescopes to scan signals from extraterrestrial life. Scientists also look for very brief flashes of light lasting only nanoseconds. However, no verifiable signs have been detected so far.

It's not very nice to be ignored!

Enough time has passed since the birth of the universe for another civilization to contact us. Why haven't we been contacted yet? Italian physicist Enrico Fermi had some thoughts on the matter.

Alien life may be so different to ours that even when we find it, we are unable to identify it.

Aliens may have not approached us because they feel it would not be beneficial to either parties.

It's possible that civilizations destroy themselves on reaching a certain point, or destroy other intelligent life.

As the universe expands, we may be too far away in space or time for aliens to reach us.

Aliens may be communicating in unknown ways but we may not be listening for the right things or for long enough.

Other civilizations may be concealing themselves or lack the advanced technology needed to communicate with us.

IMAGINATION GONE WILD

There is no hard evidence for the existence of extraterrestrial life. But news reports are filled with sightings of UFOs (unidentified flying objects). Most UFOs have turned out to be aircraft, optical illusions, or natural phenomena like sun dogs. Some people have gone so far as to say that they have met and even been abducted by aliens.

Jai Singh II

He ascended the throne at the age of 11 and ruled over Amber for 44 years. He planned the spectacular city of Jaipur and oversaw its construction. Fiercely protective of the Rajput states, he clashed with the Mughals to defend them. He introduced tax reforms and encouraged education. Yet, somehow, he found time for his passion project – astronomy. This is an imagined conversation with Maharaja Sawai Jai Singh II.

Q: I am very curious about your name. It is really unusual. What does "Sawai" mean?

A: "Sawai" is a title given to me by the Mughal emperor Aurangzeb. It implies that I am one and a quarter times superior to the other kings of my time.

Q. Speaking of superiority, you have had so many career highlights. It is tough to choose which one is the greatest, but if I had to take a pick, I would say it is your idea of building multiple observatories. Could you talk us through them?

A: I have always been curious about the universe's mysteries. I fell in love with mathematics and astronomy as a child. When I finally became king, I had the resources to explore my interests. So I commissioned five observatories, known as the Jantar Mantars, between 1724 and 1734. Jantar Mantar is a Sanskrit term and it literally means "formula of instruments". Each one consists of instruments, or yantra, made of stones »

Miniature painting of Maharaja Sawai Jai Singh II

and bricks, in various geometrical shapes and sizes. The one in Delhi was built first, followed by those in Jaipur, Mathura, Ujjain, and Varanasi.

Q: What was the motivation behind building these observatories?

A: The hand-held brass instruments used before were small, lacked division into minutes, were prone to wear and tear on their axes, and had inaccurate centres and unstable planes. Thus, they were not suitable for accurate measurements. I built the observatories to provide more precise readings of the positions and movements of the celestial bodies so as to construct almanacs in the service of religion and the State. I have also written about them in my book *Zij Muhammad Shahi.*

The Kranti Vritta Yantra, which is used to measure the latitude and longitude of celestial objects

Q: Rumour has it that you borrowed some astronomical elements from Greek and Persian observatories. Is that true?

A: That is right. They inspired me to some degree. But I am no imitator. One day, I thought to myself how much more dependable would observations of the sky become if the instruments were to be magnified and made permanent. So I adapted and added to the designs of earlier sight-based observatories and designed sturdier and larger models. The instruments one sees now at the Jantar Mantars are a lot bigger and far more complex. In fact, some of them are rather unique in design and function.

Q: That's quite a long list. Any closing thoughts?

A: I would just like to thank those who paved the way for me. It includes the Greek astronomer Ptolemy, the Uzbek astronomer Ulugh Beg, and the French astronomer La Hire. I was so inspired with their efforts that I had their works translated into Sanskrit. I could vnot have gotten as far as I did without them.

Jantar Mantar

Unique astronomical monuments, Jantar Mantars comprise massive fixed instruments built of brick and stone. In contrast to the handheld brass tools, these provide more precise readings of the positions and movements of celestial objects. Of the five observatories commissioned by Jai Singh II, the one in Jaipur, built in 1724–34, is the largest and best preserved.

UNNATAMSHA YANTRA A large circular brass ring supported by pillars and beams, it was used to determine the positions of stars and planets at any time of day or night.

NADIVALAYA YANTRA These sundials incorporate two circular surfaces parallel to the equatorial plane, with metal rods pointing towards the poles mounted at their centres. This represents the two hemispheres and calculates time by following the solar cycle.

LAGHU SAMRAT YANTRA This "small sundial" calculates the local time of Jaipur up to an accuracy of 20 seconds.

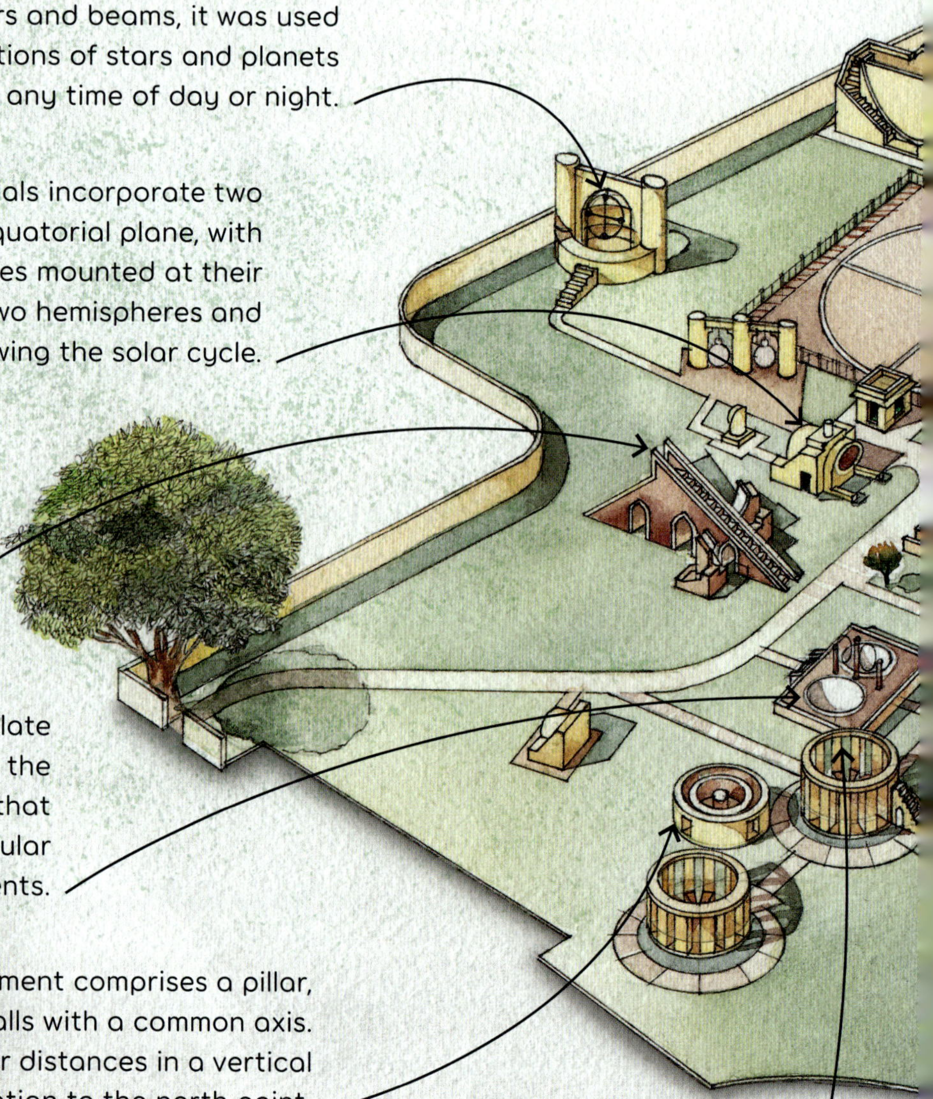

CHAKRA YANTRA Used to calculate the angles of stars and planets from the equator, it comprises a brass tube that passes through the centre of two circular metal instruments.

DIGAMSA YANTRA This instrument comprises a pillar, which is surrounded by two walls with a common axis. It is used to measure angular distances in a vertical plane in relation to the north point.

RAM YANTRA It consists of two cylindrical structures, each with a vertical column of the same height at the centre. Its primary function is to measure the altitude and azimuth of celestial objects.

SAMRAT YANTRA This is a 27-m (89-ft) high sundial with two brick quadrants on either side. It helps in measuring local astronomical time with a precision of 2 seconds and forecasting monsoon. Although it is found at all surviving observatories, it varies in size. The one in the Jaipur observatory is the world's largest sundial.

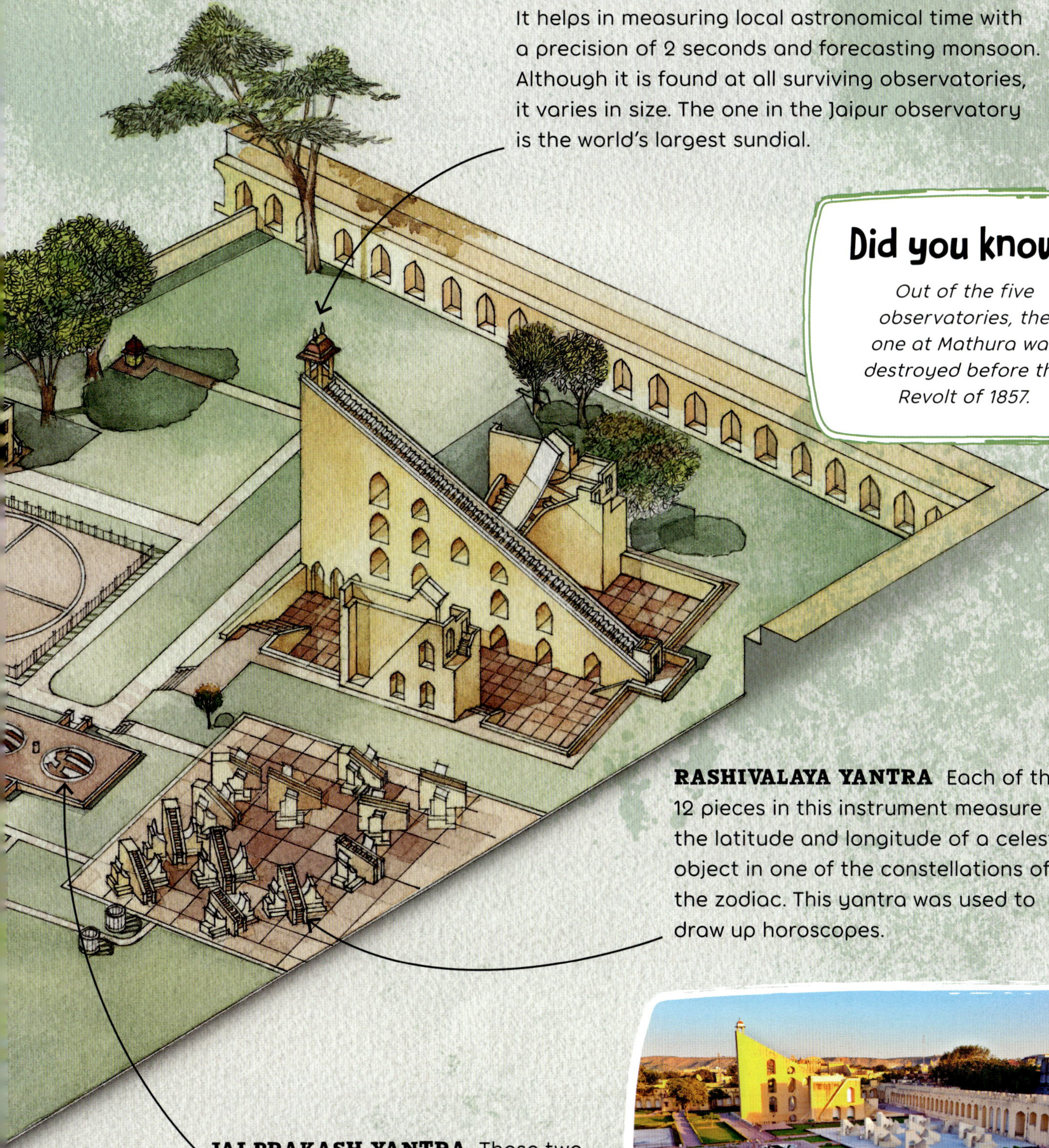

Did you know?

Out of the five observatories, the one at Mathura was destroyed before the Revolt of 1857.

RASHIVALAYA YANTRA Each of the 12 pieces in this instrument measure the latitude and longitude of a celestial object in one of the constellations of the zodiac. This yantra was used to draw up horoscopes.

JAI PRAKASH YANTRA These two concave hemispheres erected side by side produce an inverted image of the sky. The instrument could be used to read the positions of heavenly bodies by making visual alignments as well as the time of the spring equinox.

Present-day Jantar Mantar in Jaipur, Rajasthan

Early discoveries

Astronomical discoveries have trickled in ever since the first astronomers looked up at the sky and waited for things to happen. The works of astronomers, such as Nicolaus Copernicus, Tycho Brahe, Johannes Kepler, Galileo Galilei, and Isaac Newton, paved the way for many more remarkable discoveries in the 18th and 19th centuries.

HALLEY'S HOMECOMING

In 1705, English astronomer Edmond Halley noticed that three comet orbits in 1531, 1607, and 1682 were very similar. He discovered that it was actually the same comet. Halley predicted that it would be visible again in 1758. His prediction came true, but he did not live long enough to experience it. Later, the comet was named after him. It was the first object proven to orbit around the Sun other than a planet.

EXPANDING THE HORIZONS

German-born British astronomer William Herschel discovered the planet Uranus in 1781. However, he was not really looking for it. Herschel chanced upon it while looking for multiple star systems and announced that he had found a comet. Later, a group of astronomers corrected his finding and declared it a planet.

Did you know?

In 1783, English clergyman John Michel was the first to suggest the existence of black holes, which he called "dark stars".

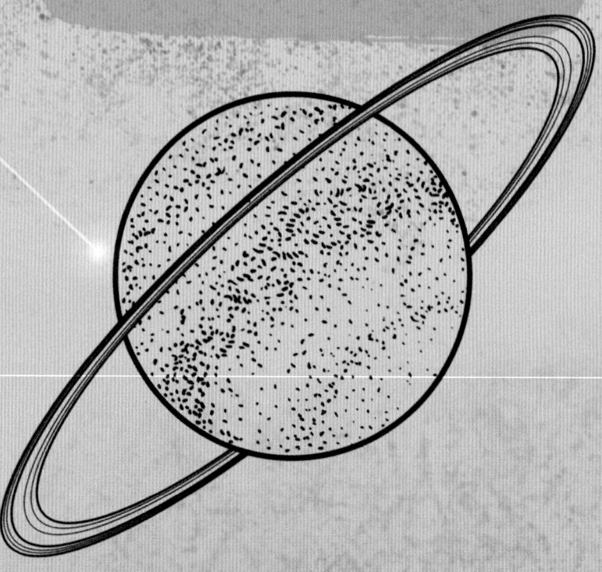

CELESTIAL POLICE REPORTING, SIR!

In 1766, German astronomer Johann Titius proposed that an unknown body occupied the gap between Mars and Jupiter. His claims were reformulated by another astronomer, Johann Bode, in 1772. In 1800, a group of astronomers, called the "Celestial Police", decided to look for this mysterious planet. Finally, in 1801, Italian astronomer Giuseppe Piazzi spotted it and named it Ceres. Later observations indicated that it was an asteroid. Then, in 2006, it was given the status of a dwarf planet – the only one in the asteroid belt.

THE OTHER BLUE PLANET

Following the discovery of Uranus, many astronomers noted irregularities in its orbit. Then came the suggestion that there could be another planet beyond Uranus. This was because most irregularities are due to the gravitational pull of another planet. French astronomer Urbain Le Verrier used Newton's law of gravity to work out this mystery and establish its possible position. He shared his findings with German astronomer Johann Galle who spotted Neptune at the predicted location in 1846.

STARLIGHT DECODED

In 1814, German scientists Gustav Kirchhoff and Robert Bunsen invented an instrument, called the spectroscope, to measure the spectrum of stars, including the Sun. Soon, they managed to isolate the spectra for many known substances. In 1868, British astronomer Joseph Norman Lockyer developed his own spectroscope to study the second layer of the Sun's atmosphere directly, which led him to the discovery of the element helium.

The quest for a sunny spot

Lush green valleys, terraced plantations, and pleasant climate makes the misty hill station of Kodaikanal, in Tamil Nadu, a popular vacation spot. But, this place is also home to one of the oldest solar observatories, set up in 1899, which has been observing the Sun for more than 115 years.

Kodaikanal Solar Observatory in the Palani Hills of Tamil Nadu

Sunspots are the cooler parts on the Sun's surface and often appear in pairs.

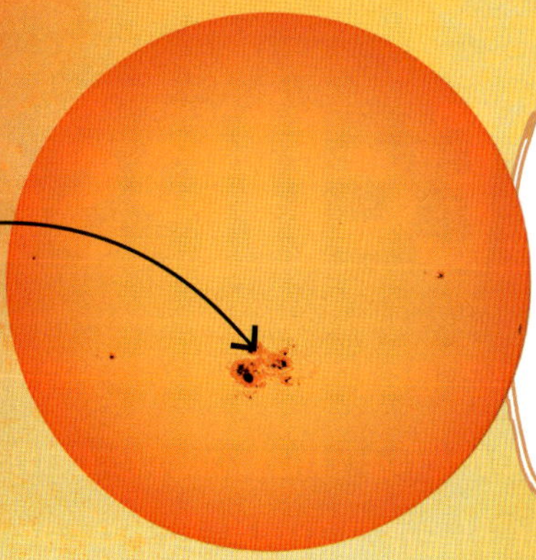

Fun fact

Dark patches on the Sun's surface are called sunspots. A single one can be bigger than the entire Earth.

BEGINNINGS

The Kodaikanal Solar Observatory was once a private observatory, set up by an officer of the East India Company (EIC) in 1787, in the Madras Presidency. The EIC later took over and operated it as the Madras Observatory. In the early 1900s, following the devastating Madras famine of 1876–77, it moved to Kodaikanal. This was because of the region's dust-free, high altitude location and the need to study monsoon patterns.

Spectroheliograph at the Kodaikanal Observatory

Did you know?

Two common filters for observing the Sun through a telescope are the Hydrogen-Alpha (red light) and the Calcium-K (blue light). One can view the Sun using specific light by blocking all other wavelengths of light passing through only a tiny part of the solar spectrum.

This equatorial mount is a part of the spectroheliograph at the Kodaikanal Observatory.

H-alpha telescope, which was installed at the Kodaikanal Observatory in October 2014

GROWTH AND PROGRESS

In the early 20th century, the observatory began regular observations of the Sun. Then, British astronomer John Evershed arrived in 1907. Two years later, he discovered the radical motion or outflow of gasses in sunspots, which became known as The Evershed Effect. The Kodaikanal Solar Observatory is today one of the most important centres for solar studies. It is one of the only three solar observatories in the world to have a comparable collection of instruments.

Eclipses

To ancient people, eclipses were unexplained, unexpected, and irregular phenomena that were considered to be bad omens. Today, we know their cause. Eclipses takes place when one celestial body moves into the shadow of another celestial body.

TYPES OF ECLIPSES

LUNAR ECLIPSE

Often, the Earth moves between the Sun and the Moon, blocking the direct sunlight that is normally reflected by the Moon. This causes an eclipse of the Moon, during which Earth casts its shadow on the Moon. Lunar eclipses can occur only when the Moon is full and are more frequent and longer than solar eclipses.

SOLAR ECLIPSE

Sometimes, the Moon moves between the Sun and the Earth, blocking the sunlight from reaching the Earth. This causes an eclipse of the Sun. During this time, the shadow cast by the Moon plunges a part of the Earth into darkness for a short while. Solar eclipses are less common and last only for a few minutes. One must remember to never look directly at the Sun as its intense light can cause eye damage. Proper equipment must be used to observe solar eclipse.

MYTHOLOGICAL INTERPRETATIONS

In mythologies of many cultures, solar eclipses involve mythical figures, often animals, on a gastronomical mission to devour the Sun. For example, in Hindu mythology, a cunning demon named Rahu is believed to have caused eclipses as he swallowed the Sun. But, it would reappear again as the demon had no body to contain it. Similarly, in Vietnam, it was believed that a solar eclipse was caused by a giant frog eating the Sun, while Norse cultures blamed wolves.

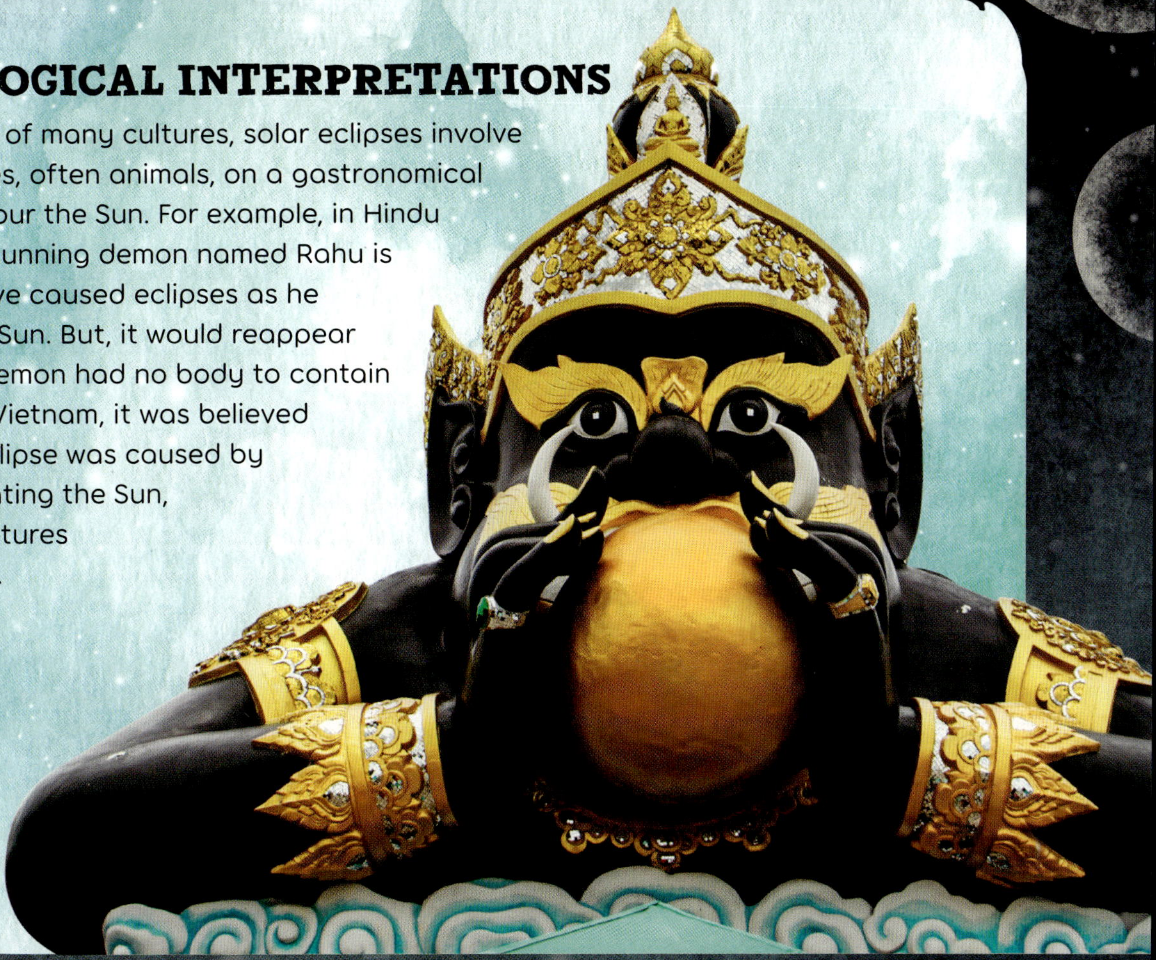

A statue of Rahu eating the Sun

Did you know?

During solar eclipses, animals and birds get puzzled. Those that are active during the day head back to their nighttime abodes while nocturnal animals think they have overslept. Some spider species break down their webs, bats come out of their caves, songbirds stop singing, mosquitoes become more active, and some flowers may even start to close up.

Sisir Kumar Mitra

Sisir Kumar Mitra learnt from some of the pioneers in the field of science and went on to become one of the leading physicists in the world. He was also the pioneer of radio science in India.

EXCELLENT TUTELAGE

Mitra was born on 24 October 1890 in the suburb of Konnagar in the Bengal Presidency. While he was young, he was inspired by Indian aeronaut Ram Chandra Chatterjee. While studying at the University of Calcutta, he worked under C V Raman and later, with eminent physicists, such as Charles Fabry, Marie Curie, and Camille Gutton.

Did you know?

A crater on the far side of the Moon is named after Mitra.

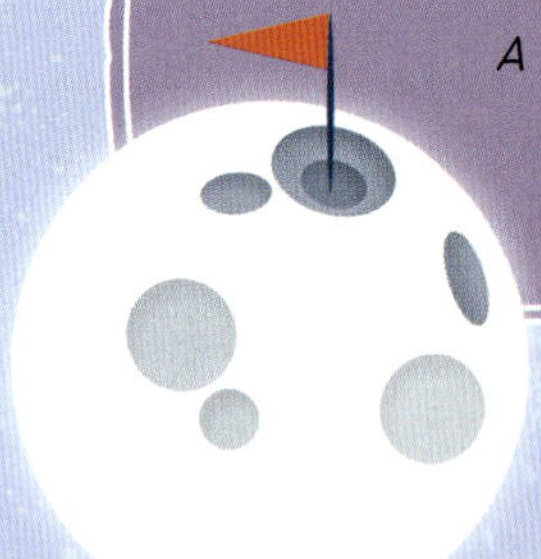

NEW AVENUES

In 1923, while teaching at the University of Calcutta, Mitra pursued research in the field of wireless communication and set up a wireless laboratory. His investigations contributed greatly to the development of radio broadcasting in India.

IONOSPHERE

Around the same time, Mitra was fascinated by another area of study – the ionosphere. He studied the effects that natural phenomena had on it and even built an instrument for measuring the heights of its different layers. He recorded his observations in his book *The Upper Atmosphere*, which was later used by the Soviet scientists for the launch of *Sputnik 1*.

Meghnad Saha

Indian astrophysicist Meghnad Saha's life was anything but ordinary. He faced many challenges, but remained undeterred. He persevered and established himself as one of the leading scientific minds of his age.

DIFFICULTIES ABOUND

Born on 6 October 1893 in Seoratali, a village in present-day Bangladesh, Meghnad Saha belonged to a lower-caste family that struggled to make ends meet and battled stereotypes and discrimination on a daily basis.

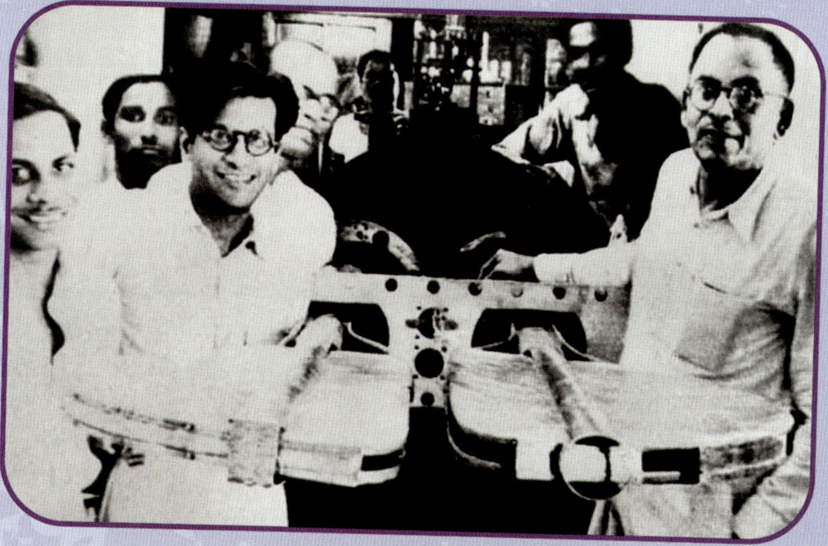

Meghnad Saha (right) and his colleagues in the lab at the Institute of Nuclear Physics

SAHA EQUATION

In 1920, Saha developed the thermal ionization equation, popularly known as the Saha equation. It gives the relationship between the temperature of a star and its spectrum, and laid the foundation for much research in the fields of astrophysics and astrochemistry. Saha also went on to invent an instrument to measure the weight and pressure of solar rays.

SCIENCE AND POLITICS

A passionate supporter of the Indian freedom movement, Saha promoted scientific knowledge to encourage nationalism. To achieve this, he set up many research institutes, including the National Academy of Science in 1930 and the Indian Physical Society in 1934. He also founded the journal *Science and Culture*, which highlighted the importance of science in society.

Did you know?

In 1952, Saha was elected as a Member of Parliament and actively worked in the fields of education, refugee and rehabilitation, atomic energy, multipurpose river projects, and flood control.

C V Raman

One of the greatest Indian scientists, Chandrasekhara Venkata Raman is known for his groundbreaking work in the field of physics. In 1930, he became the first Asian recipient of the Nobel Prize in Physics. Throughout his life, Raman promoted the growth of science in India and contributed to scientific principles applicable in many fields, including space sciences.

Did you know?

In India, 28 February is celebrated as National Science Day to mark the day Raman discovered the Raman Effect.

7 November 1888 Born at Tiruchirappalli, Tamil Nadu, to Parvathi and Chandrasekharan Ramanathan Ayyar

1903–05 Enrolls in Presidency College in Chennai, Tamil Nadu, for a bachelor's degree and graduates with a gold medal in physics and English

1907 Shifts to Kolkata, West Bengal, and begins research at the Indian Association for the Cultivation of Science (AISC)

1917 Joins Calcutta University as a professor of physics

1921–28 Observes the blue colour of the Mediterranean Sea, which later leads to the discovery of the Raman Effect

A KEEN OBSERVER

A sea voyage to London in 1921 inspired Raman to investigate the reason behind why sea water appears blue to us. At that time, English physical scientist Lord Rayleigh had explained that the blue colour was due to the reflection of the colour of the sky. However, Raman noticed that the sea did not change its colour despite an overcast grey sky. This observation prompted a series of experiments that led to the discovery of the Raman Effect. He received the Nobel Prize in Physics for this discovery.

The Raman Effect

On 28 February 1928, Raman established that when light passes through a dust-free and transparent medium, some light beams alter their wavelength while scattering. This phenomenon explains why the sea appears blue to us. It is because the colour blue has a shorter wavelength so it scatters more than other colours when light falls on water. His discovery paved the way for the science of modern optics. It is most commonly used in scanners that are used for security and medical checks.

Fun fact

A ship is named after Raman in the film Star Trek: The Next Generation, *which is part of the famous international science fiction franchise* Star Trek.

1929 Knighted by the British Government for his contribution to science

1930 Receives the Nobel Prize in Physics for his discovery of the Raman Effect

1934 Sponsors the establishment of the Indian Academy of Sciences

1936 Discovers the Raman-Nath theory with his colleague Nagendra Nath

1948 Founds the Raman Research Institute (RRI) in Bengaluru, Karnataka

1954 Receives the Bharat Ratna – the highest civilian honour in India

2 November 1970 Passes away at his home in the RRI campus

Galaxies galore

Billions of galaxies are scattered across the universe. Each galaxy is a collection of stars, gas, and dust held together by gravity. They vary a great deal in shape, size, and the type of stars within them.

A composite image of the Whirlpool Galaxy, or Messier 51, as taken from NASA's Chandra X-ray Observatory, with its smaller satellite galaxy on the left

The Antennae Galaxies – NGC 4038 and NGC 4039 – have been in a state of collision for millions of years. As they collide, huge clouds of gas appear pink and red, while star-forming regions appear blue. This image was taken by the Hubble Space Telescope.

GALAXY SHAPES

The most basic method to classify galaxies is according to their shapes. They appear in three main shapes. American astronomer Edwin Hubble devised a more accurate method. He subdivided the galaxy shapes and gave them a code of numbers and letters.

NGC 6814

SPIRAL

Some galaxies look like a whirlpool. Called spiral galaxies, they have a big, bright centre, with many arms emanating from it.

Satellite galaxies

Most of the time, smaller companion galaxies, called satellite galaxies, orbit larger host galaxies. They are bound to their host by its gravitational force.

The Andromeda galaxy is known to have many satellite galaxies.

Galaxy cluster

The gravitational pull of galaxies is so strong that they often tend to pull one another to form clusters. In this process, many galaxies collide and merge. Sometimes, they also orbit each other.

Abell 2537 galaxy cluster

Black holes

At the centre of most galaxies is a vast black hole. It is the enormous gravitational pull of the black holes that holds together most galaxies.

NGC 1300

BARRED SPIRAL

This is a subtype of a spiral galaxy. Stars in barred spirals form a bar in the centre, with spiral arms stretching out from each end of this bar.

NGC 3610

ELLIPTICAL

Appearing in simple ball shapes, elliptical galaxies don't contain much gas or dust. Thus, they hardly support new star formation.

NGC 5408

IRREGULAR

Mostly comprising gas and dust, irregular galaxies are quite rare. They have no identifiable shape, but contain numerous young stars.

Constellations

The night sky looks like it has been peppered with hundreds of thousands of twinkling stars. For the longest time, humans drew imaginary lines through these stars to find patterns in the sky. They called these constellations and named the patterns after mythical beasts and heroes.

MAPPING THE SKY

Humans grouped stars into constellations to create a handy map of the sky. The stars may appear equidistant to us, but in reality, they are very far from each other. If you were to view the night sky from a place other than the Earth, it is possible that you would notice a different pattern.

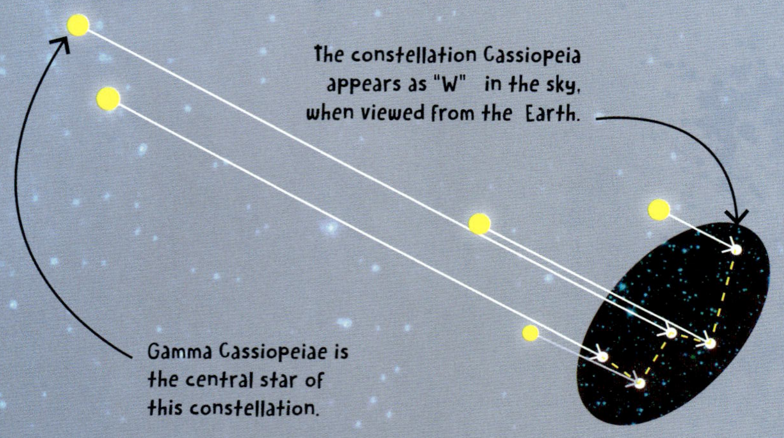

SAPTARISHI MANDAL

The great bear constellation has many names including Ursa Major, big bear, and Saptarishi. Saptarishi is a collective term for the seven great ancient Indian sages, who are praised in the sacred Vedas. They were Vashistha, Marichi, Pulastya, Pulaha, Atri, Angiras, Kratu.

SHINING BRIGHT

The constellations are drawn using the brightest stars in the sky, but this doesn't mean that these are the brightest in reality. The luminosity of stars depends on their proximity to the Earth. For example, Sirius, in the constellation Canis Major, is the brightest star in the Earth's night sky. But if it was the same distance from the Sun, it would be much bigger and brighter than the Sun.

A portion of sky near Canis Major

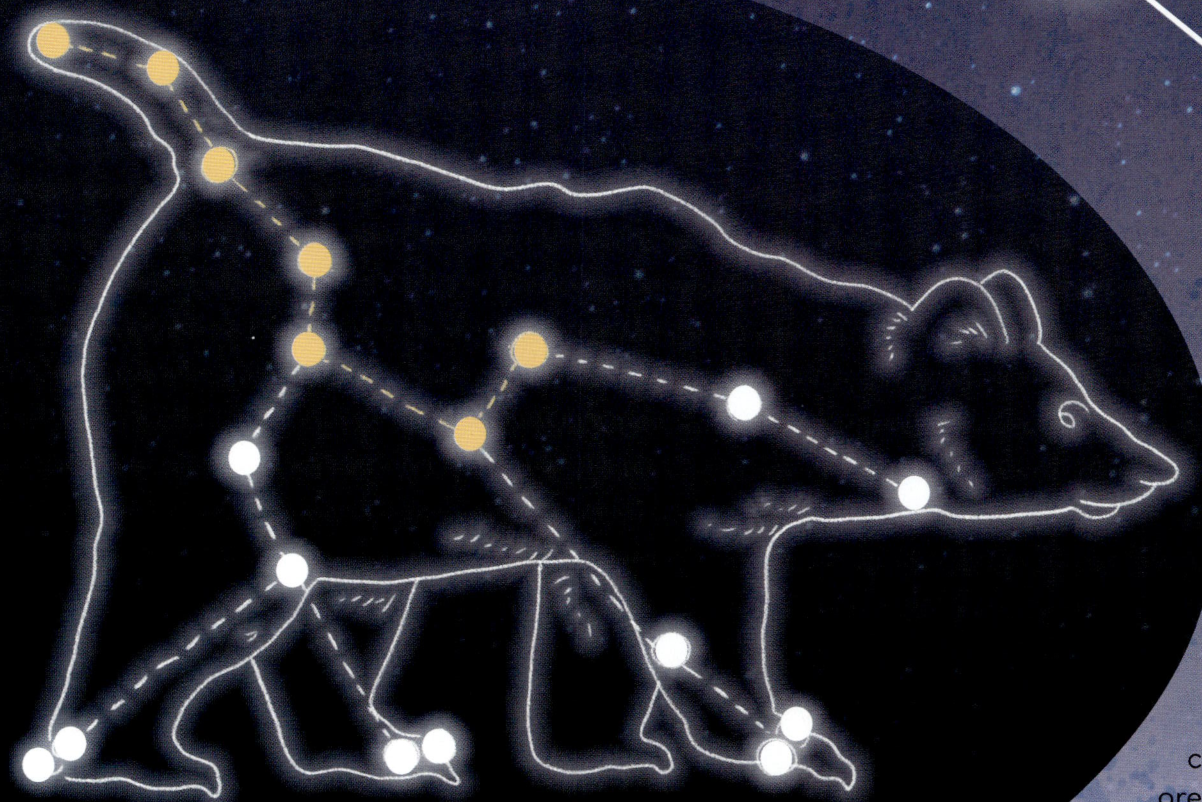

SHAPE WITHIN A SHAPE

Some stars form a recognizable pattern in the sky, but they are not grouped together as a constellation. These patterns of stars are called asterisms. They may be found in a single constellation or across constellations. The Plough in Ursa Major, or the great bear, is a popular example of an asterism.

A young India explores

The decade following India's independence from the British rule saw the country buzzing with calibre and frothing with ambition. It was ready to propel itself into a new era of discovery and exploration. But a series of questions and considerations stood between the nation and its space dream.

TOO MUCH ON OUR PLATE ALREADY?

In the late 1940s and 1950s, India was busy with a series of nation-building projects. They were all meant to help the country get back on its feet after hundreds of years of colonial rule. This included making laws, fighting social evils, building infrastructure, and focusing on regular and reliable food production. Around the time the world's first artificial satellite, *Sputnik 1*, launched, India ranked low on almost all socio-economic indicators, including literacy, gender disparity, poverty, and employment. It is why many believed that India should not even think about a space programme. The belief was that space exploration was meant for rich and elite nations, such as the USA and the USSR, and not for a developing nation, such as India.

TRY WE MUST

Some people thought differently. Indian physicists Vikram Sarabhai and Homi Bhabha believed that a space programme in India could actually assist with nation-building rather than be a burden on it. They believed that space technology would be useful in communication, remote sensing, education, and help growing industries such as agriculture and health. In fact Sarabhai claimed that space technology could help India "leapfrog" in its development mission.

"It is science alone that can solve the problems of hunger and poverty, of insanitation and illiteracy, of superstition and deadening custom and tradition, of vast resources running to waste, of a rich country inhabited by starving people."

Jawaharlal Nehru

A TRYST WITH DESTINY AND A ROMANCE WITH SCIENCE

Vikram Sarabhai and Homi Bhabha found an ally in India's first prime minister, Jawaharlal Nehru, who shared their belief that a space programme would benefit the country and helped them garner support for their mission. Their visionary thinking led India to build and launch rockets, satellites, and satellite launch vehicles, all within the first four decades of its independence.

Pillars of Creation

In 1995, the Hubble Space Telescope captured a spectacular photograph showing columns of gas and dust in the Eagle Nebula in the constellation Serpens. These huge tower-like formations are famously called the Pillars of Creation because their dust and gas is constantly collapsing to create a number of new stars. The Hubble Space Telescope, in 2014, revisited the region to capture a clearer image. In this new view in visible-light, one can see the pillars enveloped in ultraviolet light as well as the multi-coloured emissions from different chemical elements.

Homi J Bhabha

In 1957, the launch of *Sputnik 1* by the Soviet Union made headlines all over the world. Meanwhile, a talented 48-year-old scientist from Mumbai, Homi Jehangir Bhabha, did not just stop to marvel at this feat, but he saw a courageous dream. He envisioned that India too could have its own space programme.

GENIUS IN THE MAKING

Homi Bhabha was born on 30 October 1909 in Mumbai. A brilliant student, in 1927, he went to the University of Cambridge in England to pursue a course in mechanical engineering. Bhabha, however, had different interests. So after completing his degree, he decided to do a doctorate in physics, followed by research in the subject.

Did you know?

Not just science, but Bhabha took great interest in arts and literature too. Several of his paintings are displayed at TIFR.

BENEFICIAL HURDLE

In 1939, Bhabha came to India for a vacation, but was unable to return to Cambridge when the Second World War started, leading to turmoil in Europe. So he decided to stay and continue his research in India. He joined the Indian Institute of Science (IISc), Bengaluru, where he met Vikram Sarabhai – the physicist who laid the foundations of space research in India.

CHAMPION OF NUCLEAR PROGRAMME

A visionary with great foresight, Bhabha soon realized that the new republic of India needed a nuclear energy programme for power generation and future industrial growth. He played a crucial role in convincing the government to support scientific aspirations.

PAVING THE WAY

Soon, Bhabha grew dejected by the state of scientific research in the country and decided to improve the conditions. He played a pivotal role in the establishment of the Tata Institute of Fundamental Research (TIFR) and the Atomic Energy Commission. In 1962, he provided institutional support to Sarabhai in setting up the Indian National Committee for Space Research (INCOSPAR), which marked the formal beginning of the space programme in India.

A 1966 Indian stamp showing Bhabha

VISION FOR INDIA'S SPACE PROGRAMME

Bhabha donned many hats during the early years of India's space programme. He even surveyed suitable locations for the country's first rocket launch. His vision for the Indian space programme was clear – development of home-grown technology for rockets, satellites, and launch vehicles. Tragedy struck on 24 January 1966, when Bhabha died in a plane crash, while on his way to an international conference.

Bhabha Atomic Research Centre (BARC), which was founded by Bhabha in January 1954

Yuri Gagarin

The space race of the 1950s and 1960s saw the USSR and the USA jockeying to become the first nation to send a human being into space. Then, on 12 April 1961, something remarkable happened. Soviet cosmonaut Yuri Gagarin blasted off into space aboard *Vostok 1*, changing the course of history forever.

ROAD TO SPACE

Born on 9 March 1934, near Gzhatsk, Russia, Yuri graduated as a molder and eventually entered the Soviet air force. Later, he was chosen from among 154 contenders for the space mission. On the morning of the launch day, he wore his spacesuit, rode a bus to the launch pad in Baikonur, Kazakhstan, and climbed inside the tiny spacecraft carried by an R-7 rocket. "*Poyekhali!*" (Let's Go!), he yelled as the countdown began, and minutes later, he was in space.

Vostok 1 with cross section showing Yuri Gagarin

"To be the first to enter the cosmos, to engage, single-handed, in an unprecedented duel with nature – could one dream of anything more?"

IN AN UNKNOWN WORLD

The spacecraft *Vostok 1* had a cone-shaped service module which carried the engine, air tanks, fuel, and a ball-shaped descent module with Yuri in it. The spacecraft was remotely controlled by the centre on ground as officials weren't sure if Yuri would be able to operate it himself in the unfamiliar, weightless environment. They did give him special instructions on how to override the control systems in case of an emergency. The spacecraft whizzed around the Earth's orbit and, 108 minutes later, after being plunged through the atmosphere in a ballistic descent, Yuri landed safely back on Soviet soil.

Neil Armstrong

Just six weeks after the first crewed space mission, US President John F Kennedy announced that the USA would land astronauts on the Moon before 1970. At the time, it had only made one human spaceflight of 15 minutes, so the target was ambitious. This is where Neil Armstrong came in.

READY TO FLY

Born on 5 August 1930 in Ohio, USA, Neil was passionate about aviation and flight from his childhood. He fought in the Korean War and was later groomed at NASA to become an astronaut. On July 16 1969, along with Buzz Aldrin and Michael Collins, he began his trip to the Moon. Their mission was called *Apollo 11*.

HISTORIC DESCENT

Apollo 11 was carried out by two spacecraft – the command/service module called *Columbia*, and the lunar module called *Eagle*. They travelled through space locked together, but separated near the Moon. Neil and Buzz climbed into the *Eagle* and made their descent to the Moon's surface while Michael stayed in *Columbia* and travelled around the Moon.

Neil Armstrong with special camera equipment, carried on the *Apollo 11* flight

ON THE MOON

As Neil took his first steps on lunar soil, satellites beamed live images back to the Earth. There, 650 million viewers across the world, watched with their eyes glued to television screens. Neil and Buzz spent 2 hours and 48 minutes on the Moon, walking around, setting up experiments, taking photographs, and collecting rock and soil samples. They then returned to the *Eagle*, eventually rejoining *Columbia* for their journey back home.

Through the decades

The era of space travel began in the 20th century with the invention of rockets. It was followed by robotic space explorers and even habitable space stations. By the century's end, thousands of spacecraft and hundreds of people had gone to space. Throughout the history of space exploration, there were some key breakthroughs.

1940s and 1950s

1942
V-2 rocket German rocket scientist Wernher von Braun built the V-2 rocket as a weapon for the Second World War. This development proved that rockets had the potential to reach space.

1947
First animals in space The USA adapted the captured German V-2 rockets to send the first living creatures – fruit flies – into space. The mission's aim was to see how living beings would respond in space.

1957
The two Sputniks Russia launched the first human-made satellite, *Sputnik 1*, as well as *Sputnik 2*, which carried Laika, a dog, into orbit.

1959
Luna Series Soviet probe *Luna 1* became the first spacecraft to leave the Earth's gravity. It was followed by *Luna 2*, which was the first one to land. Finally, *Luna 3* gave us the first glimpse of the far side of the Moon.

1960s

1961
First man in space Soviet cosmonaut Yuri Gagarin became the first person to go to space. He orbited the Earth in less than 100 hours, in his tiny *Vostok 1*.

1963
First woman in space As the pilot of *Vostok 6*, Soviet cosmonaut Valentina Tereshkova became the first woman to go to space. She spent three days, orbiting the Earth 48 times.

1965
First spacewalk Soviet cosmonaut Aleksei Leonov performed the first spacewalk. Connected by a safety tether, he spent 10 minutes outside his spacecraft.

1966
First soft landing on the Moon by a spacecraft Soviet spacecraft *Luna 9* became the first one to land successfully on the Moon.

1969
Humans on the Moon *Apollo 11* became the first crewed mission to reach the Moon. On board were American astronauts Neil Armstrong and Buzz Aldrin who took their first steps on the lunar surface on 21 July.

1970s

1970
Lunokhod 1 Soviets launched the first lunar roving vehicle, *Lunokhod 1*. It explored the Moon's rocky surface for 11 days.

1971
Salyut 1 World's first space station launched by the Soviet Union. Its three-member crew lived in the station for 24 days, demonstrating that it was possible for astronauts to live and work in space.

1973
Skylab The first US space station went into orbit. Its crew performed nearly 300 experiments before it fell back to the Earth in 1979.

1975
Aryabhata India's first satellite launched from Russia.

1976
First spacecraft on Mars NASA's *Viking 1* was the first spacecraft to land on Mars. It spent 6 years investigating the planet.

1980s and 1990s

1981
Columbia NASA's space shuttle *Columbia* was launched. It flew 28 times and was the world's first reusable spacecraft.

1986
Mir Soviet space station *Mir*, occupied by a crew of three astronauts, was put into the Earth's orbit.

1990
Hubble Space Telescope
NASA's space shuttle *Discovery* placed the Hubble Space Telescope in orbit. Over the years, it revealed unseen distant wonders of space.

1997
***Sojourner*'s journey** NASA's *Sojourner* rover was the first wheeled lander to touch down on Mars. It operated for three months, taking more than 500 photographs.

1998
International Space Station (ISS) The construction of the *ISS* in space began. Once complete, it became the largest human-made object to orbit the Earth.

1999
PSLV's errands India's PSLV started carrying foreign payloads. It soon became a favourable carrier for various countries due to its reliability and cost-efficiency.

2010s

2001
First tourist in space American engineer and entrepreneur Dennis Tito paid 20 million dollars to spend a week aboard the *ISS*, becoming the first tourist in space.

2004
Opportunity
NASA's *Opportunity* rover landed on Mars to search for signs of past life.

2008
A lunar first ISRO sent its first mission, *Chandrayaan-1*, to the Moon.

2009
Kepler Observatory NASA launched Kepler, which used a special light-measuring device to search for planets orbiting distant stars.

2010
A private affair
Virgin Galactic flew the first suborbital plane and SpaceX put a spacecraft into orbit and returned it to the Earth safely.

2020s

2012
Curiosity NASA's *Curiosity* rover landed on Mars. It found that Mars could have supported life earlier.

2014
Comet landing A robotic device detached from the *Rosetta* space probe made the first soft landing on a comet, called 67P. The same year, ISRO launched its *Mars Orbiter Mission*.

2015
First private spacecraft to the *ISS* SpaceX's first commercial spacecraft, *Dragon*, delivered supplies to the *ISS*.

2009
Chinese victory China's *Chang'e-4* landed on the far side of the Moon.

2020
New discoveries NASA launched its Mars-bound *Perseverance* rover.

2021
"Going private soon" Virgin Galactic independently launched a civilian into space.

Nowhere but forward
In the coming years, space research is likely to continue the hunt for distant planets that might harbour life. A crewed mission to Mars by 2050 may be a reality.

From INCOSPAR to ISRO

When the USSR launched the world's first artificial satellite *Sputnik*, it left Vikram Sarabhai eager for India to have its own space agency. Thus began the dream of ISRO in the mind of its founding father, who eventually transformed it into a vision, a plan of action, a raison d'être, and finally a reality.

FINDING OUR FEET

During the first decade following Independence, Vikram Sarabhai led the Physical Research Laboratory (PRL) while Homi J Bhabha oversaw the Department of Atomic Energy (DAE). Determined to make India space-bound, the two scientists began research on space technologies. Prime Minister Jawaharlal Nehru was keen on exploring the field as well, so it was easy for the two to secure funding. In 1961, the government set up the Space Research and the Peaceful Uses of Outer Space department under the DAE and officially recognised PRL as the designated research centre for space science. The game was afoot and there was no looking back.

Vikram Sarabhai

Homi J Bhabha

Physical Research Laboratory (PRL), Ahmedabad, Gujarat

KALPATHI RAMAKRISHNA RAMANATHAN

Among the lesser-known people who helped propel ISRO to great heights is K R Ramanathan. A physicist and meteorologist, he was the Director of the Physical Research Laboratory (PRL) and played a crucial role in setting up the launch station in Thumba. His studies on the upper atmosphere, conducted through rocket launches, paved the way for future research.

BABY STEPS

To kick-start India's space programme, Sarabhai and Bhabha needed help. They decided to approach NASA for help with setting up a sounding rocket station and a tracking station to communicate with satellites.

By 1962, it was agreed that NASA would provide rockets for a sounding rocket project and train Indian scientists. India would assemble a team, procure equipment for performing experiments, and set up a launch station.

The same year, the Indian National Committee for Space Research (INCOSPAR) was founded and led to the establishment of the Thumba Equatorial Rocket Launching Station (TERLS).

UP AND RUNNING

By the middle of the 1960s, INCOSPAR's mission was in full swing. Resources were difficult to come by, so they used whatever was at hand. So, bicycles and bullock carts transported rocket parts.

In the next few years, the team grew and eventually the space programme constituted a whole government department in itself.

In 1969, the Indian Space Research Organisation (ISRO) was born. Today, it has a network of several research centres spread across the country.

Shining moments

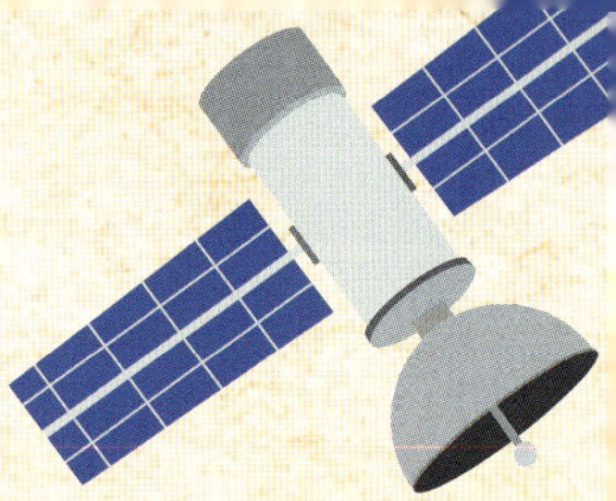

From carrying rockets on bicycles to reaching Mars in its first attempt, there have been many milestones in India's journey across space.

1963
The launch of the first sounding rocket from Thumba Equatorial Rocket Launching Station (TERLS) marked the beginning of India's space programme.

1975
ISRO and NASA, in a joint mission, carried out an experimental satellite communications project, called the Satellite Instructional Television Experiment (SITE). It made informational television programmes accessible to rural parts of India. The same year, India launched its first satellite, *Aryabhata*, from the Soviet Union.

1979
India's first Earth observation experimental satellite, *Bhaskara I*, was launched. It was the first satellite to feature cameras.

1981
The Ariane Passenger Payload Experiment (*APPLE*) was the first Indian experimental geostationary communication satellite. In the same year, *Bhaskara II* was also launched with some improvements.

1982
A US rocket launched India's first meteorology satellite, the *INSAT-1A* communication satellite. The INSAT satellites have provided communication services well into the 21st century.

1984
Squadron leader and cosmonaut Rakesh Sharma became the first Indian to go to space. He was part of an Indo-Soviet crewed mission and spent almost eight days aboard the Russian space station *Salyut 7*.

1988
The first operational Indian Remote Sensing (IRS) satellite, *IRA-1A*, was launched from the Soviet Union. The IRS series heralded the coming of age of Indian satellites.

India's first satellite *Aryabhata*

Scale models of *Chandrayaan-2's* orbiter

1994
The year marked the successful launch of Polar Satellite Launch Vehicle (PSLV). It became a favoured carrier for satellites of various countries because of its cost efficiency and reliability.

2004
EDUSAT, a dedicated education satellite, the first of its kind, was launched. It was designed to facilitate education initiatives.

2008
The country witnessed its first mission to the Moon. Called *Chandrayaan-1*, its objective was to send back data and images of the entire lunar surface. The second lunar mission, called *Chandrayaan-2*, followed in 2019.

2013
Mars Orbiter Mission (*MOM*) spacecraft, or *Mangalyaan*, went into space, marking India's first interplanetary mission. This made it the first country to reach Mars in its maiden attempt.

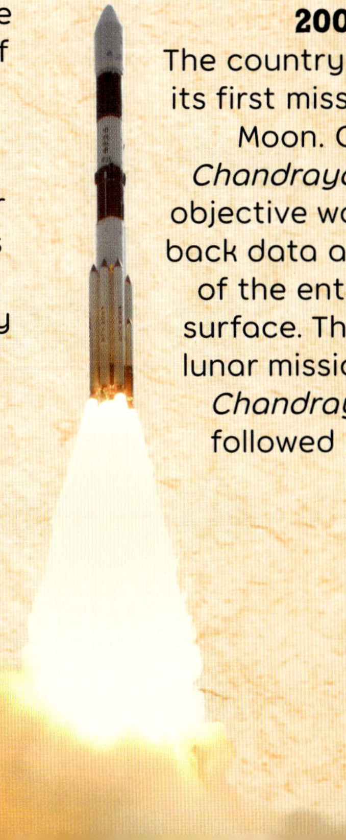

Launch of the *Mars Orbiter Mission*

2016
India tested its first indigenous Reusable Launch Vehicle (RLV) in a demonstration launch.

Reusable Launch Vehicle-Technology Demonstrator (RLV-TD)

2017
India rocked the world when it launched an Earth observation satellite and 103 co-passenger satellites all at once.

Scale model of *Chandrayaan-2's* rover

Who's who in space

Since the beginning of the Space Age in the 1950s, government space agencies have led the space exploration programmes in their countries. Although initially, there was a tussle between the countries to get ahead in space exploration, in the recent years, many of them are collaborating with each other in a quest to unravel the mysteries of the unknown world.

NASA

Created in 1958, the US space agency, National Aeronautics Space Administration (NASA), became the first to send astronauts to the Moon. Its success pushed the other countries to create their own space agencies. Since then, NASA has sent probes to Saturn, Jupiter, Pluto, and the Sun, and even a rover on Mars.

ESA

Efforts towards space exploration in Europe were consolidated in the 1950s and 1960s, following the efflux of European scientists to the USA and the USSR. The European Space Agency (ESA) was founded in 1975. Over the years, it has undertaken joint missions to Saturn, Mars, and Mercury, besides being an active participant in the Hubble Space Telescope and the James Webb Space Telescope.

Did you know?

The European Space Agency (ESA) has 22 countries from Europe and Canada in its organization.

ROSCOSMOS

The Russian Federal Space Agency, established in 1992, emerged from the Soviet space programme of the 1950s. It pioneered space exploration in the latter half of the 20th century, with many notable firsts in its legacy, such as the first satellite, the first human in space, and the first space station.

CNSA

Established in 1993, the China National Space Administration (CNSA) is the first agency to achieve a soft landing on the far side of the Moon. After NASA, it is the second agency to land a rover on Mars. It is also constructing its independent space station in the low Earth orbit (LEO).

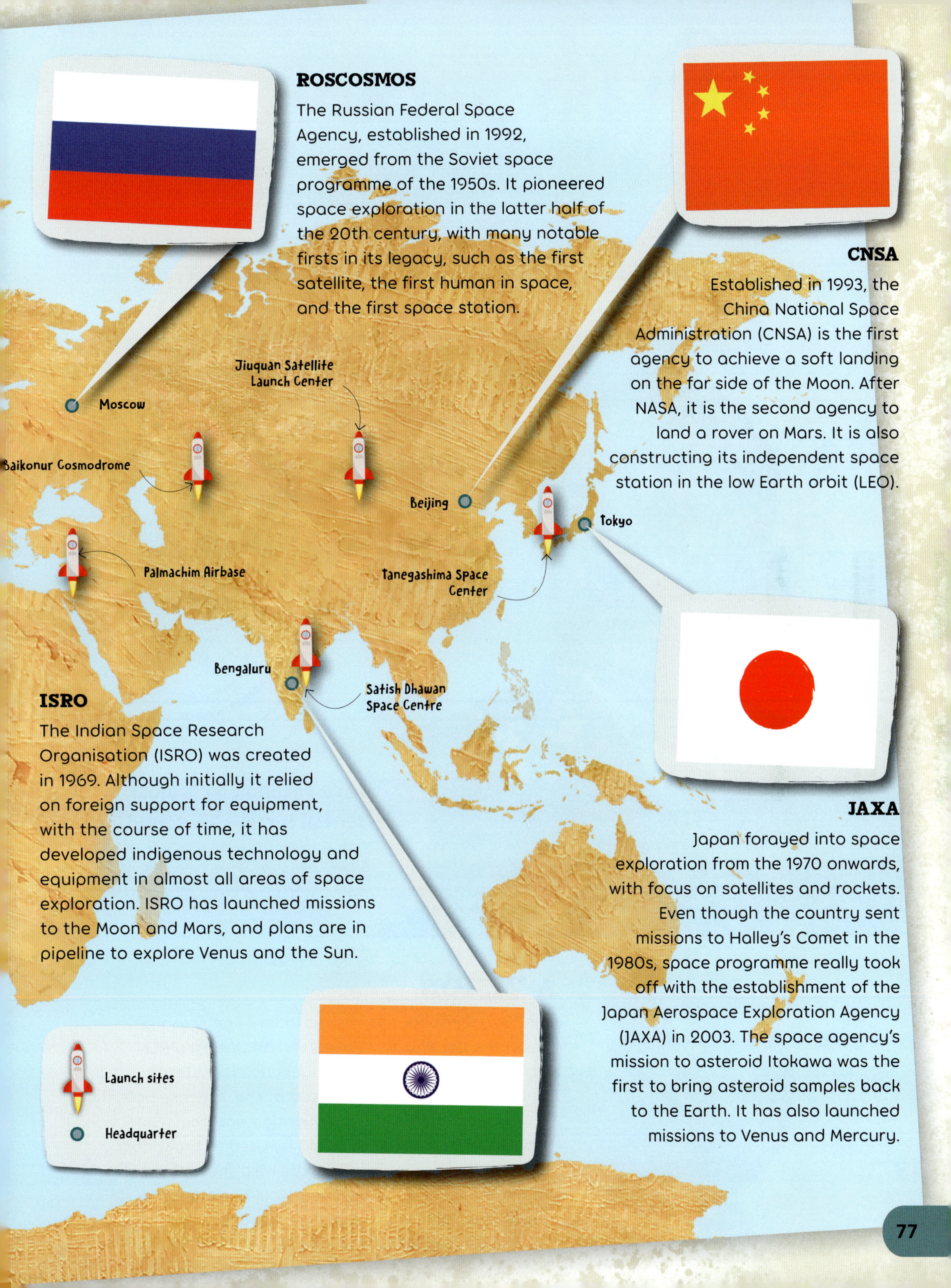

ISRO

The Indian Space Research Organisation (ISRO) was created in 1969. Although initially it relied on foreign support for equipment, with the course of time, it has developed indigenous technology and equipment in almost all areas of space exploration. ISRO has launched missions to the Moon and Mars, and plans are in pipeline to explore Venus and the Sun.

JAXA

Japan forayed into space exploration from the 1970 onwards, with focus on satellites and rockets. Even though the country sent missions to Halley's Comet in the 1980s, space programme really took off with the establishment of the Japan Aerospace Exploration Agency (JAXA) in 2003. The space agency's mission to asteroid Itokawa was the first to bring asteroid samples back to the Earth. It has also launched missions to Venus and Mercury.

Vikram Sarabhai

Physicist Vikram Sarabhai recognized that science and space technology had the potential to place India on the path of development and success. Considered the architect of the Indian space programme, he was the force behind the establishment of some of the country's most important institutions, including the Indian Space Research Organisation (ISRO) that helms India's space research and exploration.

"Space technology is most essential for the all-round economic development of India."

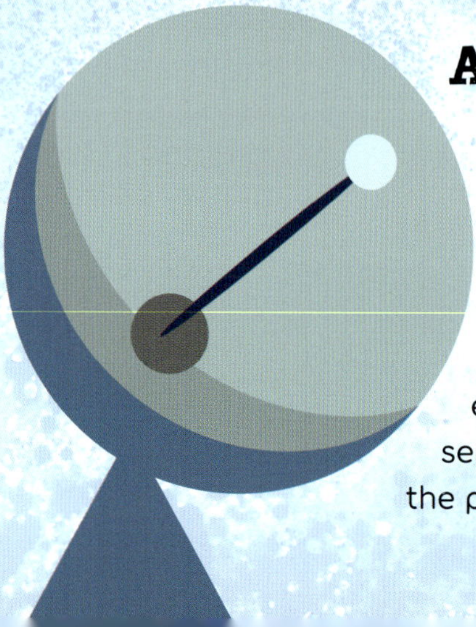

A VISION

In 1947, Sarabhai established India's first research centre, the Physical Research Laboratory (PRL). Ten years later, the USSR launched its satellite, *Sputnik*. Sarabhai, convinced of the immense potential of space technology in education and communication, believed that satellites could be used to broadcast educational programmes across rural India. Remote sensing technology, he believed, would help address the problems of a newly independent country.

THE BEGINNINGS

In 1962, Sarabhai wrote to the Prime Minister Jawaharlal Nehru asking him to set up a space programme. It led to the establishment of the Indian National Committee for Space Research (INCOSPAR).

Sarabhai with Kalam in the early days of ISRO

ISRO has today become India's national space agency

A DREAM REALIZED

He worked with Homi Bhabha to set up India's first rocket station in Thumba, Kerala. In 1969, INCOSPAR was renamed Indian Space Research Organisation (ISRO). It was here that Sarabhai helped build India's first satellite, *Aryabhata*, that went into space in 1975 – four years after his death.

TEACHING INDIA

Sarabhai also collaborated with foreign space agencies, specifically NASA in the 1970s. This was to use their satellites to broadcast educational programmes to more than 5,000 Indian villages. This became known as the Satellite Instructional Television Experiment (SITE).

An ISRO technician with TV model designed with NASA's help

Did you know?

A crater on the Moon at the Sea of Serenity has been named Sarabhai crater in his honour.

TERLS

Soon after the establishment of INCOSPAR in 1962, Vikram Sarabhai and his team of scientists began looking for a site to set up a rocket launch pad station. Their search led them to the sleepy little village of Thumba in Kerala. It stood on the Earth's magnetic equator, making it an ideal spot for conducting atmospheric research.

GOD'S ABODE

The magnetic equator ran through the site of the 400-year-old church of St Mary Magdalene and the team approached the bishop to obtain the land to build a rocket launch station. The bishop asked Sarabhai's team to attend the Sunday Mass at the church. There, he asked the congregation, "My children, can we give the God's abode for a scientific mission?" A unanimous "Amen" rang through the church, and with that, the Thumba Equatorial Rocket Launching Station (TERLS) was set up.

A 1969 picture of Nike-Apache being prepared for launch

BUILDING ROCKETS

Soon, work began at TERLS for assembling NASA's Nike-Apache rocket, which became the first rocket to be launched from India. The prayer room, with the untouched altar and the statue of St Mary Magdalene, was used for assembly. The bishop's quarters served as the first design and drawing office, while various other wings of the church were used as temporary accommodation for the scientists.

INTERNATIONAL RECOGNITION

In the 1960s, TERLS became an important centre for scientific confluence. It received support from the USA, the UK, the Soviet Union, France, and West Germany in the form of technical equipment, such as telemetry receivers, tracking systems, and computers. In 1965, the UN General Assembly passed a resolution to sponsor the facility, marking TERLS's place on the world stage. In return, India dedicated the centre to the UN as a goodwill gesture in 1968.

Vikram Sarabhai addressing a gathering to mark India's dedication of TERLS to the UN

TERLS TODAY

In the last 50 years, TERLS has launched thousands of rockets, which include those of Indian origin and those from other countries such as the USA, Russia, Japan, France, and Germany. St Mary Magdalene's church is now a museum where visitors can learn about ISRO's history. Elaborate exhibits describe everything, from famous Indian space missions to the inner components of a rocket. The Polar Satellite Launch Vehicle (PSLV) in the church's garden is a popular attraction.

Space exploration

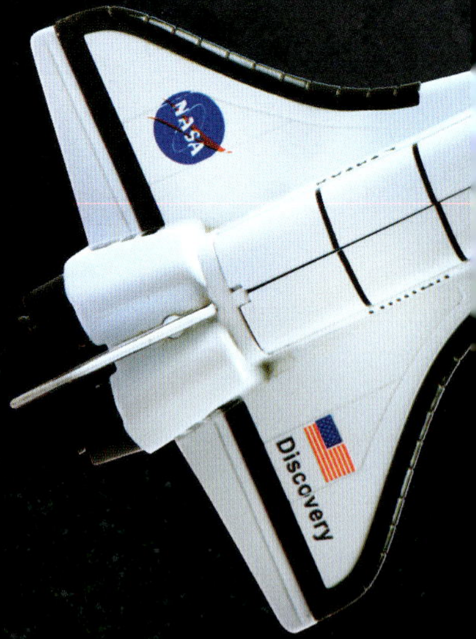

The launch of the first satellite in the 1950s ushered in a new era of space exploration. Since then, astronauts have walked on the Moon, robotic spacecraft have explored the outer reaches of the solar system, and giant telescopes have allowed scientists to peer across the vast distance of the universe.

WHAT IS A SPACECRAFT?

It is a vehicle that functions in a controlled flight route above the Earth's lower atmosphere. Most spacecraft depend on the velocity of launch vehicles to send them into space. There, the spacecraft separates from the launch vehicle to either orbit around the Earth or go to another destination.

UNCREWED SPACECRAFT

Controlled by computers, this kind of spacecraft doesn't carry astronauts. Instead, they are packed with instruments that help study the space and its elements.

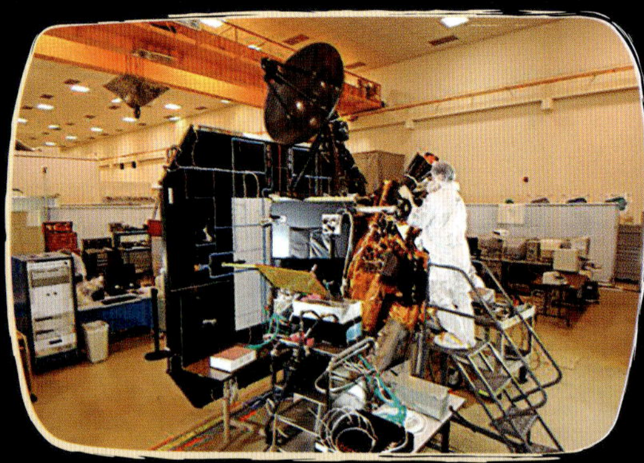

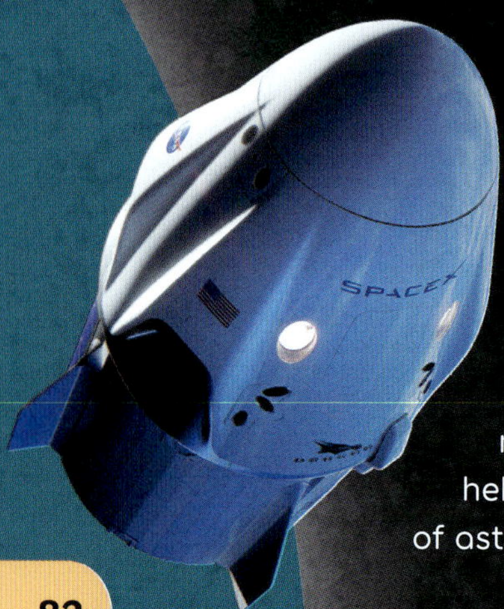

CREWED SPACECRAFT

Initially, crewed spacecraft were tiny, with room only for a few astronauts who could fly for a short while. Later, new technology developed to help spacecraft carry a group of astronauts for many days.

FLYBYS

Used in initial survey missions, a flyby follows a trajectory, far away from its target to not be captured by its gravity. It does not slow down or change direction as it can only pass by their targets once.

ORBITERS

This kind of spacecraft goes slightly closer to the target than a flyby. An orbiter is designed to slow down at the right time to insert itself into the target's orbit. It provides a more in-depth look at the target.

PENETRATORS

Designed to hit its target at high speed, penetrators enter the surface of the celestial body. They are built to survive high impact for measuring and for telemetry purposes.

ARTIFICIAL SATELLITES

An object that orbits another is called a satellite. They could be natural, such as moons, or artificial, meant for communication, surveillance, navigation, or data collection.

SPACE STATION

A space station is a type of crewed satellite, a kind of orbiting laboratory in which astronauts and scientists live and work for extended periods of time. Several countries joined forces to build the *International Space Station* (*ISS*).

SPACE OBSERVATORIES

An observatory spacecraft is put in the Earth's orbit to make scientific observations of targets in great distance, devoid of the blurring effects of the Earth's atmosphere.

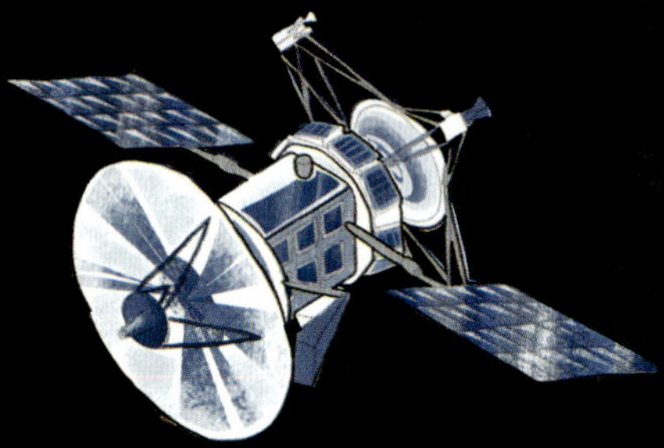

ATMOSPHERIC PROBES

This spacecraft provides information about a planet or satellite's atmosphere. Usually, it is carried by another spacecraft and requires power supply and communication equipment to relay details.

LANDERS

These spacecraft reach the surface of the target object. They are stationary and carry out missions such as testing the soil, rocks, and weather conditions. The data is sent back through radio transmissions.

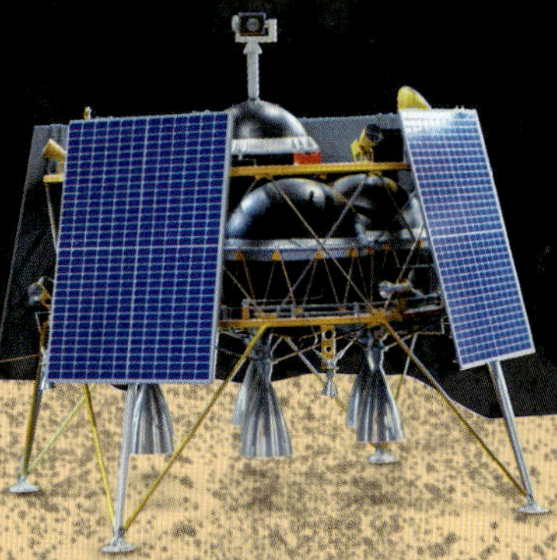

ROVERS

Unlike landers, rovers are mobile and built to travel across the surface of a planetary object on wheels. They can be autonomous or semi-autonomous.

Satish Dhawan

Mathematician and space scientist, Satish Dhawan is most well-known for leading India's space programme in the 1970s. An important part of the scientific community, Dhawan also pioneered research in other fields, such as civil aviation. He firmly believed that the application of science and technology had immense potential in improving the lives of people in India.

EARLY SUCCESS

Born on 25 September 1920, Satish Dhawan was fascinated by space even as a child. He graduated from the University of Punjab, Lahore, with degrees in diverse fields, such as mathematics and physics, English literature, and mechanical engineering. He later moved to the USA to pursue higher education in aeronautics and aerospace. When Dhawan returned to India, he started teaching at the Indian Institute of Science (IISc) and went on to become its director in 1962.

Did you know?

Dhawan set up the first supersonic wind tunnel in India at IISc.

PSLV-C47 during lift-off

ISRO's *INSAT-4B*, launched in 2007

AT THE HELM OF ISRO

After the sudden death of ISRO's chairperson Vikram Sarabhai, Dhawan took up the role in 1972. The ambitious path set by Sarabhai led him to three major projects. The first was the Satellite Instructional Television Experiment (SITE), the second was building and launching India's own satellite launching vehicle (SLV-3), and the third was the fabrication and launch of the country's first satellite, *Aryabhata*. Dhawan led these projects to completion.

CONTINUED LEGACY

Dhawan had the same goals for the space programme as Sarabhai – to make it relevant for society. Some of his focus areas included rural education and satellite communication. His efforts resulted in the operational systems, such as the telecommunications satellite INSAT, the Indian Remote Sensing (ISR) satellite, and the Polar Satellite Launch Vehicle (PSLV) that placed India in the league of space-faring nations.

Satish Dhawan Space Centre, Sriharikota, Andhra Pradesh

How satellites work

A satellite is anything that orbits a planet. Our Moon, for example, is a natural satellite. But in 1957, the Soviet Union astonished the world by sending the first artificial satellite into space. Since then, scientists world over have created many artificial satellites that help in carrying out various automatic tasks.

IN THE ORBIT

Powered by solar panels that catch intense sunlight, satellites are launched by rockets and are released at the correct height to stay in orbit. Since they orbit at the same speed as that of the Earth's rotation, they always stay over exactly the same spot.

SAT ANATOMY

Most commercial satellites are built to be as strong and light as possible. A platform, called a bus, contains all the main systems, such as batteries, computer, and thrusters. Attached to it are antennas, solar arrays, and payload instruments that the satellite uses to do its job.

SPYING

Many advanced countries in the world operate spy satellites. These advanced satellites are used to track communications, intercept electronic signals, give early warnings of missile attacks by detecting heat from missile exhausts, and take high-definition photographs of targets

WEATHER WATCH

Mapping and radiation equipment in satellites can monitor weather conditions worldwide. While geostationary satellites stay above the same place on the equator and constantly monitor one region, polar orbit satellites pass over the Earth's poles and observe every place twice a day.

THE BIG PICTURE

Some satellites specialize in taking photographs. They collect information from the Earth by recording short- and long-term changes. In this way, they can monitor agricultural activities, deforestation, groundwater movement, building constructions, forest fires, floods, and pollution.

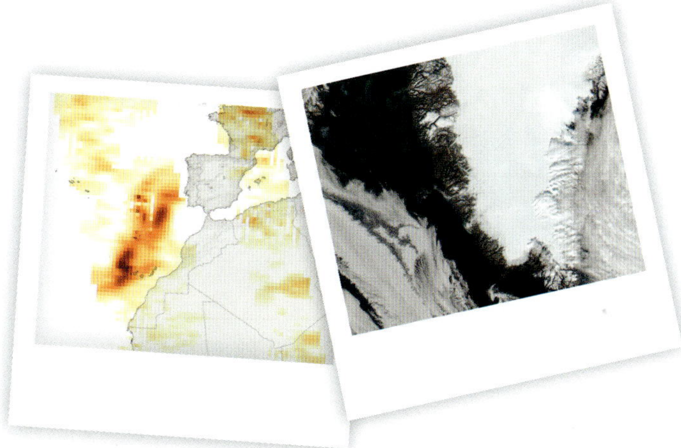

KEEPING IN TOUCH

Many artificial satellites are designed for communication, including TV broadcasts and mobile phone signals. A large one can relay more than 100,000 phone calls and 1,600 TV channels. Satellite owners can keep track of it using dish-shaped antennas on the ground as well as on the satellite.

SPACE JUNK

Wherever we humans go, we seem to leave rubbish in our wake. Space is no different. There are more than 500,000 pieces of junk orbiting our planet. These include bits from used rockets and broken satellites, and even tools that astronauts may have lost during spacewalks. Hurtling around the Earth, space junk has the potential to damage the space station and the satellites.

India's first satellite

The story of *Aryabhata* is packed with twists and turns. In the late 1960s, plans were afoot to develop satellite technology in India. Vikram Sarabhai's student U R Rao was appointed to oversee the programme. The immediate challenge lay in the mechanics of sending a satellite into space when India did not possess its own launch vehicle. The Soviets came to the rescue and the country's first satellite made its way into space.

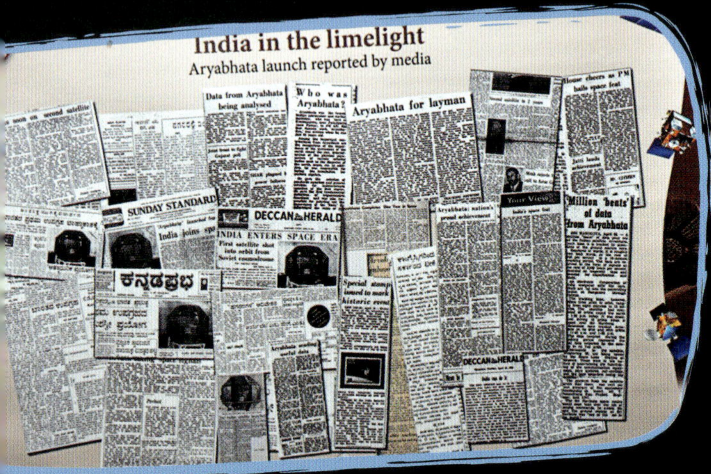

Arayabhata's launch in media reports

PACT WITH THE SOVIETS

The solution came in a letter from the Indian Ambassador to Moscow to Prime Minister Indira Gandhi. It said that the Soviets were keen to help India with its first satellite launch. During this time, both India and the USSR had tense relations with China. So the Soviets placed a condition that India's satellite would have to be heavier than China's *Dongfanghong I* satellite.

BUILDING THE DREAM PROJECT

U R Rao chose the Peenya industrial estate in Bengaluru, Karnataka, as the site for building the satellite. Makeshift sheds served as laboratories and control rooms, and a toilet was converted into a data receiving centre. India was responsible for the design, assembly, and testing of the satellite while the Soviets provided solar panels, battery, a tape recorder, and took charge of the launch.

Udupi Ramachandra Rao

Born in 1932 in Karnataka, U R Rao began his career as a cosmic-ray physicist. Besides spearheading the *Aryabhata* project, he oversaw the development of more than 20 other satellites for communication, meteorological services, and remote-sensing, including the two Bhaskara satellites. A recipient of the Padma Bhushan and Padma Vibhushan – two of the highest civilian honours of India – he is fondly remembered today as "India's Satellite Man".

THE SHINING ARMOUR

The satellite was named after Indian astronomer Aryabhata and was more than double the weight of *Dongfanghong I*. It was built in the shape of an oblate spheroid, with 26 faces made up of solar panels. It was decided that *Aryabhata* would carry three scientific payloads to conduct experiments in X-ray astronomy, measure gamma rays from the Sun, and explore the Earth's upper atmosphere.

READY, GET SET, GO!

On 19 April 1975, in a historic launch, *Aryabhata* took to the skies from the Kapustin Yar Cosmodrome launch site in the USSR. It successfully took its place in its designated orbit and travelled around the Earth for four days before suffering an electrical failure. But, it still remained in orbit for nearly 17 years.

Fact File

Weight 360 kg (794 lb)
Cost Rs 30,000,000
Launch date 19 April 1975
Launch site Kapustin Yar Cosmodrome, USSR
In orbit 17 years

Early experiments

Almost five decades ago, Indian physicist Vikram Sarabhai's vision set in motion a remarkable chain of events. The legacy of his dream – to adopt technology for the aspirations of a young nation – endures to this day.

SITE

ISRO decided to use foreign satellites to see if a satellite system could contribute to national development. In 1975, it launched the **Satellite Instructional Television Experiment (SITE)**, using the American communication satellite *ATS-6* (*Applications Technology Satellite-6*). It marked India's first attempt at using space technology to provide informal education in rural areas and was called the largest communication experiment in the world. Although a foreign satellite was used, the hardware was designed and made in India.

SITE was in operation from August 1975 to July 1976. ISRO scientists successfully broadcast educational content to 2,400 villages in the states of Andhra Pradesh, Bihar, Madhya Pradesh, Karnataka, Odisha, and Rajasthan. They were given a direct broadcast receiving set, developed at SAC in Ahmedabad, Gujarat. The main objective of the experiment was to understand how satellite television could be beneficial for mass education.

Villagers watching a TV programme as a part of SITE

The programmes, produced by the All India Radio, covered many fields, such as agriculture, family planning, and education. The project was also supported by many agencies of the United Nations.

TV sets being assembled for SITE

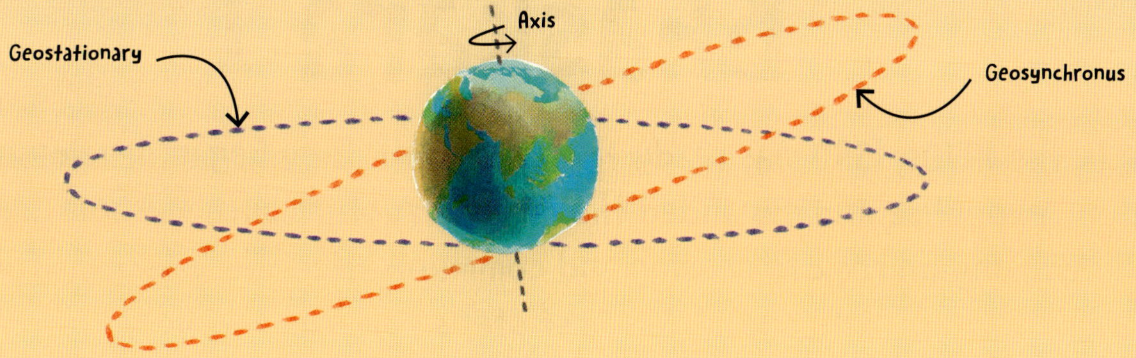

STEP

SITE was followed by ISRO's **Satellite Telecommunication Experiments Project (STEP)**, which was in collaboration with the Post and Telegraphs Department (P&T). It used the Franco-German satellite *Symphonie* and was in operation from 1977 till 1979. The project was intended as an experiment that would give inputs for a system test of using geosynchronous satellites for ground-based telecom networks, improving the competence and experience for building ground facilities, and providing experience for making an operational domestic satellite system.

What did we learn?

SITE and STEP were invaluable in providing experience to Indian space scientists for satellite applications. This, in turn, helped them make best use of the National Satellite System, the INSATs, when they were commissioned in the 1980s. Today, the INSATs and GSATs (Geostationary Satellites) are the cornerstone of India's extensive telecommunication and meteorological network.

Indian Navigation System

The Indian Regional Navigation Satellite System (IRNSS), renamed NavIC (Navigation with Indian Constellation), is the regional geo-positioning system designed by ISRO to provide accurate positioning in India and around the Indian mainland, much like the US-based GPS or the Russian GLONASS.

IRNSS-1D integrated onto PSLV-C27

Bhaskara I

In the 1970s, ISRO was ready to experiment. They began developing their expertise and expanded their infrastructure with the sole aim of focusing on remote sensing and communication. The *Bhaskara I* project was one of the first steps towards this goal.

PAST PERFECT CONTINUOUS

Two days after the launch of its first satellite, *Aryabhata*, on 19 April 1975, India signed an agreement to launch another satellite from the USSR. To save time and reduce cost, it was decided that the available spare hardware from *Aryabhata* would be used and that the second one would be the same as the first in its shape and size. It was christened after the 7th-century mathematician and astronomer Bhaskara I.

A 1984 Soviet stamp showing Bhaskara series satellites and *Aryabhata*

OPERATIONS IN SPACE

The first experimental remote sensing satellite built in India, *Bhaskara I* was also India's first low orbiting observation satellite. It was tasked with collecting data on hydrology, oceanography, and forestry. It had two slow scan television cameras and a microwave radiometer (SAMIR) for the observation of atmosphere and the ocean. This satellite was placed in orbit by a Soviet launch vehicle in 1979.

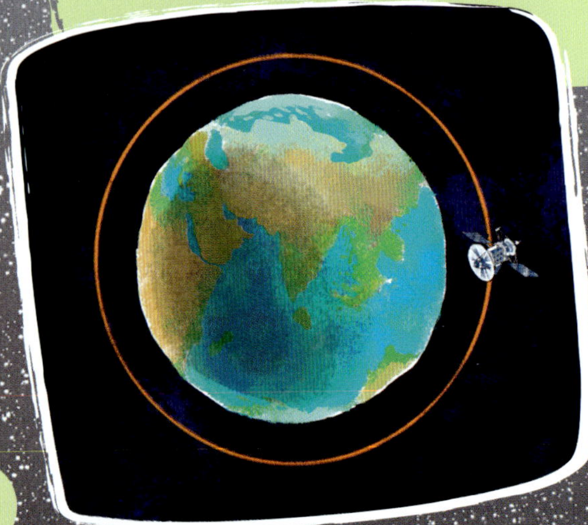

Satellite in low Earth orbit

Fact File

Satellite type Earth observation

Weight 442 kg (974 lb)

Launch date 7 June 1979

Launch site Volgograd Launch Station, USSR

In orbit About 10 years

BLIND BUT NOT DUMB

Once in orbit, all satellite systems and SAMIR performed properly. But, a trapped air bubble in the high voltage supply of the system didn't allow the camera to function for close to a year. On 16 May 1980, one of the two cameras started functioning and it beamed back an image of a cloud formation over the Bay of Bengal. Thus, Indian space imaging was born.

NO LESSONS GO WASTED

Bhaskara I was followed by *Bhaskara II* with an improved SAMIR instrument and better equipped cameras. Named after the 12th-century astronomer, *Bhaskara II* took off in the same launch vehicle from the USSR on 20 November 1981. It re-entered the Earth's atmosphere in 1991 and collected a lot of information about land and water zones and sent back around two thousand images. Many precautions were taken to ensure that the faults that crippled *Bhaskara I* would not be repeated. *Bhaskara II* was expected to lay the necessary groundwork for the setting up of a national resources survey and a management system.

Launch of Rohini

On 18 July 1980, India became the sixth country after the USSR, the USA, France, Japan, and China to have independently launched a satellite. But this triumph did not come without its set of trials and tribulations.

Rohini-1 (RS-1) satellite, which weighed 35 kg (77 lb)

HIGH AMBITIONS

In 1969, Indian physicist Vikram Sarabhai persuaded the government to establish ISRO, and oversaw the building of the nation's first launch site at Sriharikota in Andhra Pradesh. The plan for creating an Indian Satellite Launch Vehicle (SLV) was soon put in motion. The project was called SLV-3.

GEARING UP

For a whole decade, ISRO's scientists worked hard, conducting research and preparing equipment. They were led by Satish Dhawan, who had taken over as ISRO Chief after Sarabhai's death in 1971, and APJ Abdul Kalam, who was the mission's project manager. Equipped with 250 sub-assemblies, 44 major subsystems, and about a million components, SLV-3 was a groundbreaking project that would earn India a permanent position in the Space Age.

D–DAY

On the morning of 10 August 1979, carrying the *Rohini-1* (*RS-1*) satellite, SLV-3 took off for its first experimental flight. Things seemed to be going as per plan as it shot through the skies. But, 317 seconds into flight, and the rocket, along with its payload, came plummeting down and fell right into the Bay of Bengal. Things had spiralled out of control due to a nitric acid leak.

SWEET, SWEET SUCCESS

Spirits ran low at ISRO for a while, but it was essential to make a comeback soon. A second launch was planned the following year, on 18 July 1980. When the day arrived, the atmosphere in the control room was tense. At 8:03 AM, SLV-3 lifted off from Sriharikota Range (SHAR) for the second time. Within minutes, the *Rohini-1* satellite was placed in orbit. SLV-3 had performed better than expected – *Rohini-1* had been placed in an even higher orbit than planned.

Celebrations erupted in the control room and across the entire nation. People began to wonder if India would now enter into the space race and the missile race. However, ISRO's objective was clear – it would use its success to further scientific research and focus only on the peaceful use of outer space, just as the founding fathers Sarabhai and Homi Bhabha had envisioned.

Rakesh Sharma

In 1984, Indian Air Force pilot Rakesh Sharma became the first Indian to go to space. His journey captured the imagination of millions of Indians. It is the defining moment for most Indians when they think of India and space.

WINGS OF DESIRE

Born in Patiala, Punjab, Rakesh Sharma joined the Indian Air Force as a pilot in 1970. During the India–Pakistan War of 1971, he flew 21 combat missions, and rose to the position of a squadron leader in 1984.

The Soviet Union released this stamp in 1984 to mark the Indo-Soviet space collaboration.

INDO-SOVIET MISSION

In 1980, as part of Interkosmos, a Soviet initiative to helps its allies with space missions, Soviet leader Leonid Brezhnev offered to send an Indian to space. Through Project Pawan, the Indian government looked at the Indian Air Force for candidates. Many rigorous rounds later, Rakesh Sharma was selected to be the first Indian to go to space.

AMONG THE STARS

In 1984, Sharma and two Soviet cosmonauts – commander Yury Malyshev and flight engineer Gennady Strekalov – went into space aboard the *Soyuz T-11* spacecraft. They spent nearly eight days aboard the *Salyut 7* space station and conducted several biomedical experiments. They even tested to see if yoga could lessen disorientation in space.

THROUGH THE LENS

While on the *Salyut 7*, Sharma spent time photographing India. The images helped scientists map the country's natural resources. Through his powerful camera, he even spotted a group of mountaineers trying to climb the Mount Everest and alerted Myanmar authorities about a forest fire.

Retired astronaut Rakesh Sharma with a model of the Geosynchronous Satellite Launch Vehicle Mark III in Ahmedabad, Gujarat

Did you know?

When Sharma was in space, Prime Minister Indira Gandhi asked him what India looked like from up there. Quoting from a popular patriotic song, he replied, "Saare jahaan se accha" *(the best in the whole world).*

Predicting cyclones

Disaster management organizations often rely on satellites to predict and locate natural disasters, such as cyclones. High-resolution satellite images are used to create maps to predict the trajectory of the cyclone and where it would make landfall. In this image from 2020, a tropical cyclone, called Amphan, can be seen heading towards West Bengal and Bangladesh. Its constant monitoring through satellites helped in timely evacuation of millions of people. Before and after satellite images supported authorities in identifying damaged embankments, roads, and croplands.

Life in space

To live in space means to carry out everyday activities in microgravity, where everything floats and appears weightless. Even after two decades of experience in the *International Space Station* (*ISS*), there are several challenges that astronauts face, from maintaining their body weight to brushing their teeth.

WHAT'S ON THE MENU?

Special meals, designed by food scientists, are delivered to astronauts in sealed packages. All they need to do is add water. The food can't be crumbly, since it could float around and damage spacecraft equipment.

STAYING HYDRATED

Water availability is limited on the *ISS*. So wastewater, such as urine, sweat, and moisture from breath, is collected, filtered, and reused. Astronauts have said that this recycled water is cleaner than tap water on the Earth.

Did you know?

In 2001, the fast-food chain Pizza Hut sent up a vacuum-sealed salami pizza to the ISS *via a Russian rocket. This space food delivery cost $1 million.*

FITNESS IS KEY

As astronauts float in space, their muscles and bones can weaken from lack of use. To prevent this, they must exercise and maintain their strength. Thus, the *ISS* has a gym with many machines, including a treadmill and a stationary bike.

SNOOZE TIME

Weightlessness prevents astronauts from lying down on a bed to sleep. They have to zip themselves up in sleeping bags and use body straps so that they do not float around while they rest.

WHEN NATURE CALLS

Using the loo in space is usually messy and can take up to an hour. Flushing with water is impossible, so the toilet seat uses suction to pull waste into it. A funnel machine, similar to a vacuum cleaner, is used for peeing. To poop, one must sit strapped very precisely over the toilet bowl, which is fitted with a waste-collection bag.

Toilet seat that was installed on the Russian space station Mir.

KEEPING CLEAN

Astronauts use a no-rinse cleaning solution and sponges to clean themselves, followed by a towel dry. Edible toothpaste is used for brushing. As there is no bathroom sink, astronauts have to spit into a wash cloth.

Fun fact

Memorabilia carried to space includes family photographs, organizational flags, t-shirts, books, tablets, laptops, musical instruments, and even Halloween costumes.

The satellite effect

India made great strides in satellite technology, a journey that began in the 1970s by learning how to build the system. Towards the end of the 20th century, India began working on experimental, observational, communication, and scientific satellites.

ROHINI SERIES

Satellite type Experimental and Earth observation
Duration 1980–84
Number of satellites launched Four

Three out of four Rohini satellites were successfully placed in orbit. While *RS-1* was India's first indigenous satellite launch, the camera aboard the last one, *RS D-2*, provided valuable data for classifying ground features, such as water and forests.

APPLE

Satellite type Experimental
Duration 1981–83
Number of satellites launched One

The *Ariane Passenger Payload Experiment* (*APPLE*) was the first indigenously built communication satellite. It was used to conduct multiple experiments, such as national relay of radio networking and TV programmes.

BHASKARA SERIES

Satellite type Earth observation
Duration 1979–91
Number of satellites launched Two

This series included a set of two remote sensing satellites. *Bhaskara II* was instrumental in providing valuable experience in building and operating a remote sensing satellite system.

INSAT SERIES

Satellite type Communication and Earth observation

Duration: 1982–Present

Number of satellites launched 24

The Indian National Satellite (INSAT) system is one of the largest domestic communication satellite systems in the world. These multi-purpose satellites continue to provide telecom services, meteorological observations, and countrywide radio and television broadcasting.

SROSS SERIES

Satellite type Scientific and exploration

Duration 1987–94

Number of satellites launched Four

Stretched Rohini Satellite Series (SROSS) was developed for remote sensing and upper-atmosphere monitoring. Launched by the developmental flights of ASLV, the first two were unsuccessful in achieving orbit, but the others detected Gamma-ray bursts and studied the Earth's upper atmosphere.

An Ariane 5 rocket, carrying *INSAT-3D*, taking off from the Guiana Space Center in 2013

IRS SERIES

Satellite type Earth observation

Duration 1988–Present

Number of satellites launched 31

India's remote sensing programme was established in 1988 with the commissioning of *IRS-1A*, the first of the series of indigenous remote sensing satellites. These satellites helped the country manage and monitor its natural resources across industries. For example, *IRS-P4* (OCEANSAT) was launched in 1999 specifically to monitor oceans and assist fishermen in coastal waters. Now, India has one of the world's largest collection of remote sensing satellites.

ISRO's powerhouses

The successful launch of the *Rohini* satellite by an India-made launch vehicle in 1980 was an important stepping stone for the Indian space programme. It gave scientists the confidence to develop a repertoire of sophisticated launch vehicles. Today, they range from the tiny sounding rockets to the giants PSLV and GSLV.

SOUNDING ROCKETS

These are used to explore the atmosphere and conduct meteorological studies. India imported these in the beginning, but started building its own from 1965. The first was the Rohini Sounding Rocket series, which kicked off the launch vehicle programme.

SATELLITE LAUNCH VEHICLE-3 (SLV-3)

First launched in 1979, the SLV was a basic vehicle with the ability to carry a small payload to low Earth orbit (LEO). The vehicle was powered by solid fuel and carried the Rohini satellites. It was decommissioned in 1983 in favour of a more powerful and better performing rocket.

AUGMENTED SATELLITE LAUNCH VEHICLE (ASLV)

An improvement on the SLV, the ASLV had a higher range and payload capacity at low cost. Its new feature, two strap-on boosters, gave it greater power. It was used to launch the Stretched Rohini Satellite Series (SROSS) from 1987 to 1994.

POLAR SATELLITE LAUNCH VEHICLE (PSLV)

The first rocket to be equipped with liquid propellant-fuelled stages, the PSLV was developed to carry remote sensing satellites to low-altitude polar orbit. With an unmatched reliability, it is popularly called "the workhorse of ISRO". Both *Chandrayaan-1* and *Mangalyaan* were launched by a PSLV.

WHY IS THE USE OF LAUNCH VEHICLES IMPORTANT?

Enormous power is required to overcome the Earth's gravity and travel into space. So satellites and spacecraft are propelled by launch vehicles that have rocket engines and their own fuel supply. Each launch vehicle is built in stages, or parts, with their own engines that fall away, leaving the smaller, lighter vehicle to carry on the journey.

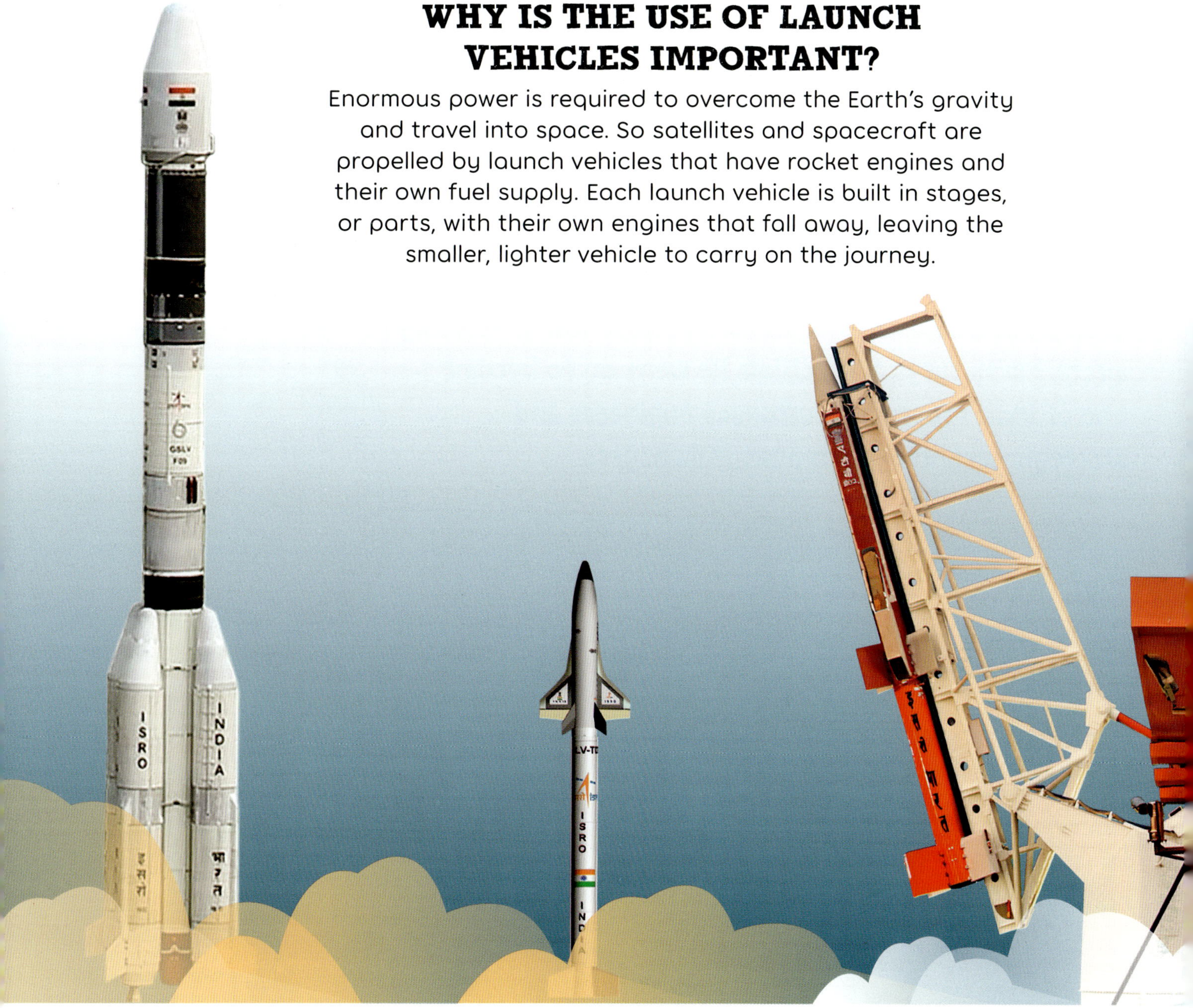

GEOSYNCHRONOUS SATELLITE LAUNCH VEHICLE (GSLV)

The GSLV programme was started in the 1990s. Developed to reach circular geosynchronous orbit (GSO), these rockets were used to launch INSAT series satellites. GLSV Mark III is the most powerful launch vehicle to be made by ISRO and was used for launching *Chandrayaan-2*.

REUSABLE LAUNCH VEHICLE - TECHNOLOGY DEMONSTRATOR (RLV-TD)

Developed to draw multiple flights out of a single rocket, the RLV has the complexity of a launch vehicle as well as an aircraft. It will also bring down the cost of placing a kilogram of payload into orbit. In future, it will become the first Indian reusable two-stage launch vehicle. Its first successful flight was tested in 2016.

SCRAMJET ENGINE - TECHNOLOGY DEMONSTRATOR

With the use of scramjet engine, launch vehicles can be lighter, faster, and cost effective. Since it creates combustion by using oxygen in the atmosphere, launch vehicles would not have to carry the gas. Successfully tested in 2016, scramjet engines can also augment ISRO's reusable launch vehicle (RLV).

APJ Abdul Kalam

Avul Pakir Jainulabdeen Abdul Kalam grew up in the quiet town of Rameswaram in Pamban Island, in southern India. He excelled in maths and science at school and studied aeronautical engineering at the Madras Institute of Technology (MIT). It is here that his interest in the world of flight transformed into a passion, as he learnt to design aircraft with surgical precision. He went on to become one of India's foremost aerospace engineers and strategic technology programme managers.

Kalam was behind the development of India's famous Prithvi and Agni missiles

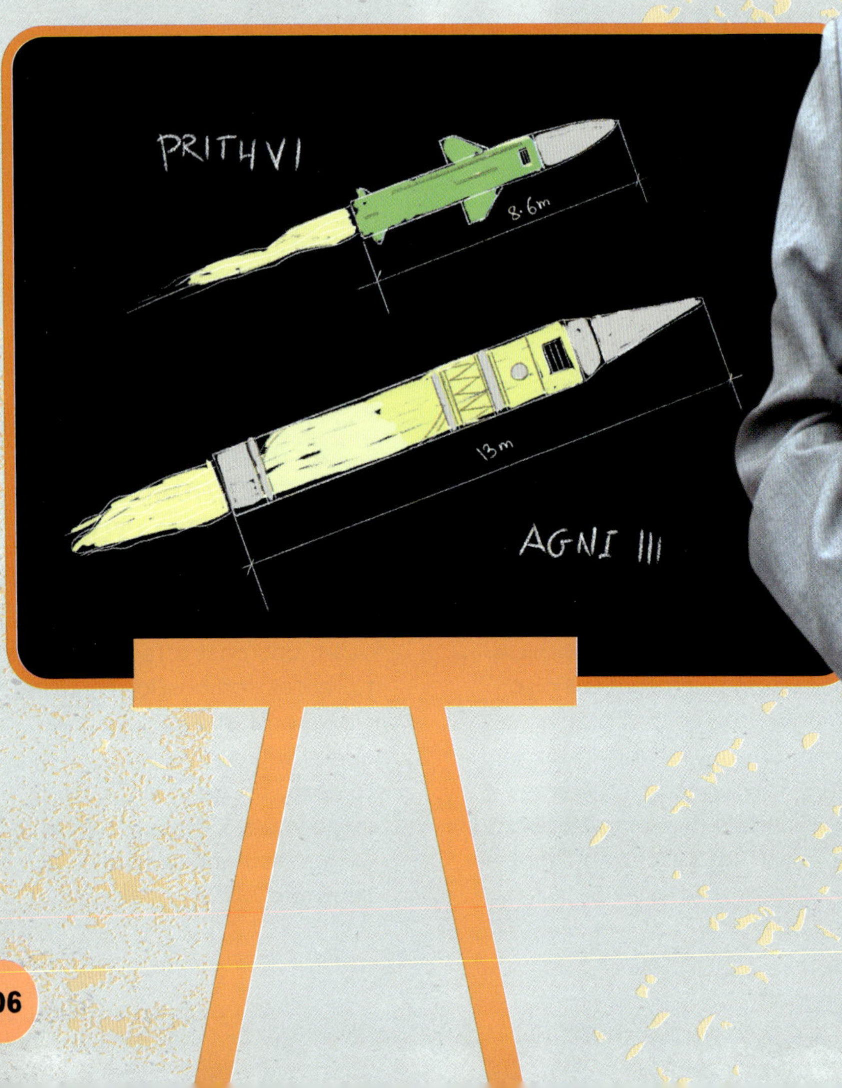

Did you know?

NASA has named a bacterium discovered on the International Space Station (ISS), Solibacillus kalamii, in honour of Kalam.

THE SKY IS NOT THE LIMIT

In the early 1960s, he joined INCOSPAR as a rocket engineer. It was everything he had ever dreamt of. He was involved in the establishment of the Thumba Equatorial Rocket Launching Station (TERLS) and his first lab was the church's prayer room. He later attended a training programme at NASA where he learnt about the launch techniques of a sounding rocket.

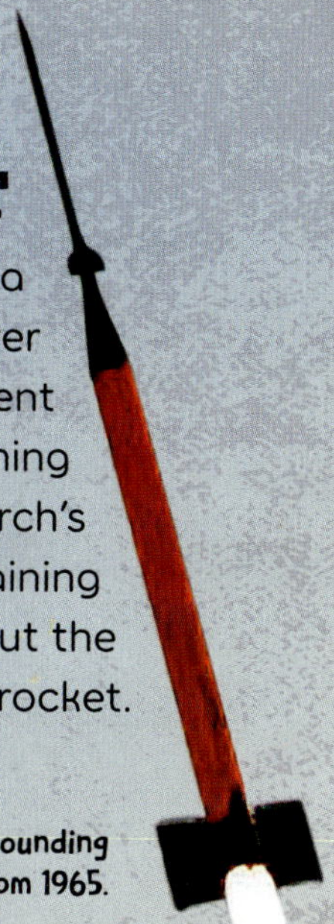

ISRO launched indigenous sounding rockets from 1965.

TAKE-OFF

Kalam's biggest triumph lay in developing India's first satellite launch vehicle – the SLV-3. In July 1980, as the SLV-3 lifted off from Sriharikota Range and placed the satellite in an orbit, there were celebrations all around. India had joined the small, elite group of nations that could launch satellites.

HEIGHT OF SUCCESS

After working on the space programme, Kalam joined the Defence Research and Development Laboratory as its director in 1982. There, he gave shape to India's ballistic missile and nuclear weapons programme. He was awarded India's highest civilian award, Bharat Ratna, in 1997. In 2002, after his retirement, he took office as the President of India. It was the first time that a scientist had held such a position.

Kalam's successful work on the missile programme earned him the moniker "Missile Man".

ISRO's workhorse

The Polar Satellite Launch Vehicle (PSLV) earned its moniker "ISRO's workhorse" based on its exceptional performance, unparalleled success, reliability, and cost-effectiveness. The PSLV has continuously made headlines around the world for international collaborations, such as its record-breaking 39th mission.

WHAT IS IT?

A PSLV is an operational ISRO vehicle launcher with four alternating solid and liquid stages that can reach multiple orbits, carrying payloads from 1,000 kg (2,205 lb) to 1,600 kg (3,527 lb).

HOW DOES A PSLV WORK?

There are four engines on this launch vehicle, which function one after the other. Also known as stages, this mechanism propels the rocket ahead to the point where it can deploy the satellite in its required orbit. Once that is done, the satellite goes on its journey ahead alone. There are four stages or parts of a PSLV.

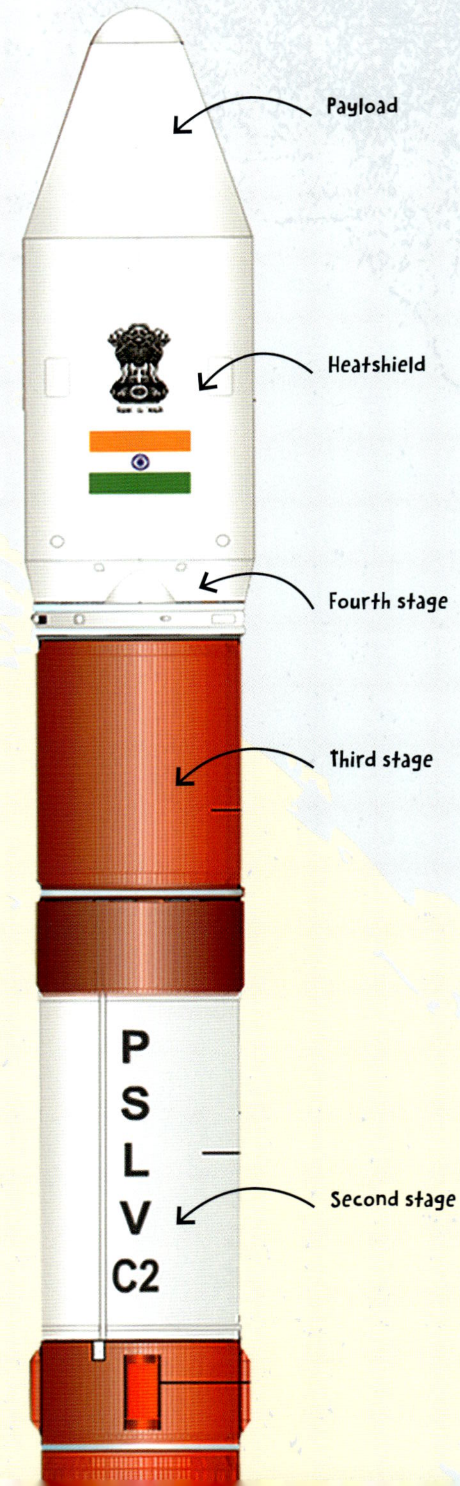

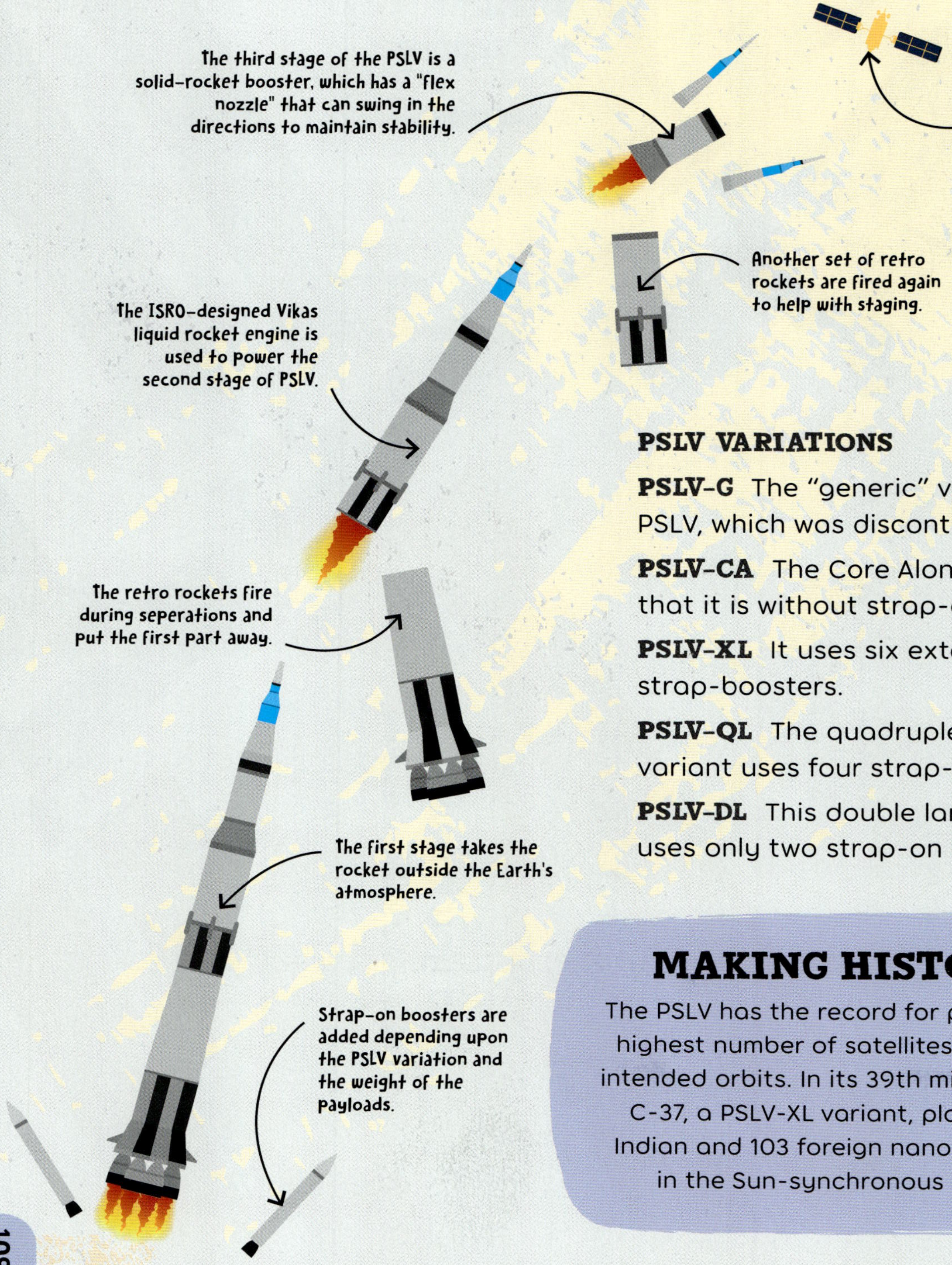

PSLV VARIATIONS

PSLV-G The "generic" version of PSLV, which was discontinued.

PSLV-CA The Core Alone (CA) denotes that it is without strap-on boosters.

PSLV-XL It uses six extended strap-boosters.

PSLV-QL The quadruple large (QL) variant uses four strap-on boosters.

PSLV-DL This double large (DL) version uses only two strap-on boosters.

MAKING HISTORY

The PSLV has the record for placing the highest number of satellites into their intended orbits. In its 39th mission, PSLV C-37, a PSLV-XL variant, placed one Indian and 103 foreign nano payloads in the Sun-synchronous orbits.

Our base in space

Soaring high above the Earth since 1998 is a spacecraft the size of a football pitch. For more than two decades, it has been a home to astronaut crews and a gigantic laboratory for research into what happens in microgravity. Called the *International Space Station* (*ISS*), it is the most ambitious project in the history of space exploration.

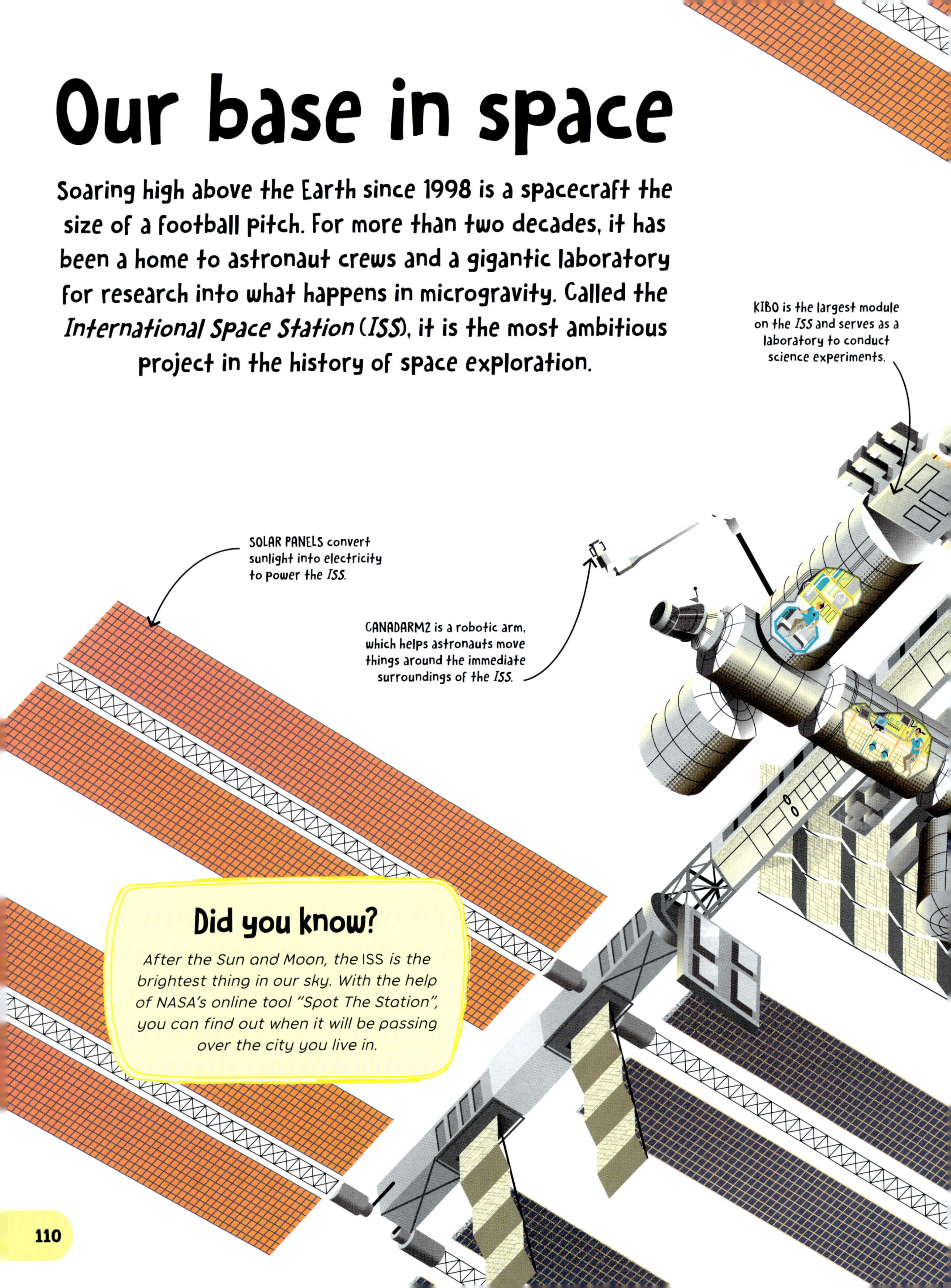

Did you know?

After the Sun and Moon, the ISS is the brightest thing in our sky. With the help of NASA's online tool "Spot The Station", you can find out when it will be passing over the city you live in.

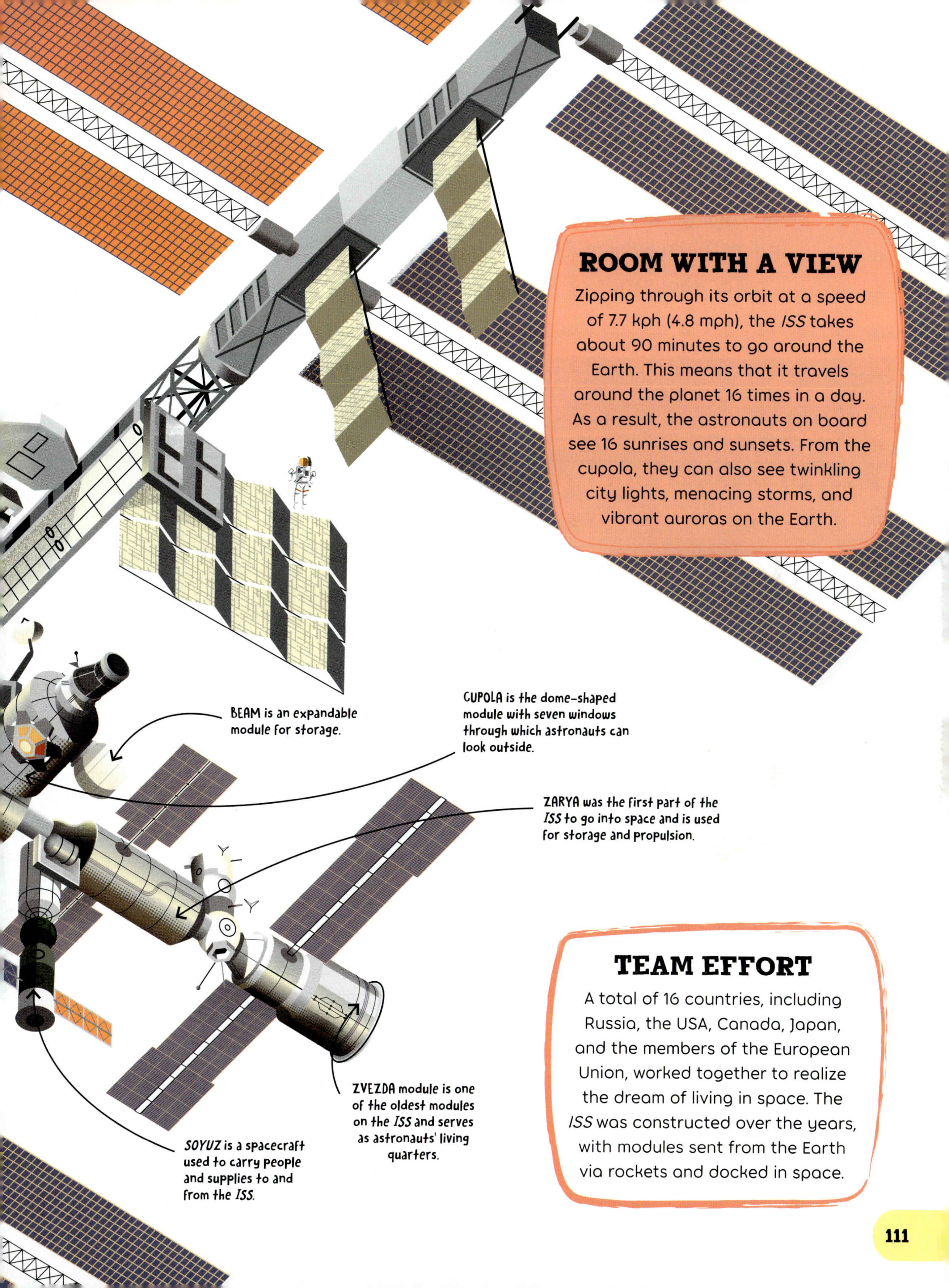

ROOM WITH A VIEW

Zipping through its orbit at a speed of 7.7 kph (4.8 mph), the *ISS* takes about 90 minutes to go around the Earth. This means that it travels around the planet 16 times in a day. As a result, the astronauts on board see 16 sunrises and sunsets. From the cupola, they can also see twinkling city lights, menacing storms, and vibrant auroras on the Earth.

TEAM EFFORT

A total of 16 countries, including Russia, the USA, Canada, Japan, and the members of the European Union, worked together to realize the dream of living in space. The *ISS* was constructed over the years, with modules sent from the Earth via rockets and docked in space.

Kalpana Chawla

As a child, Kalpana Chawla wanted to explore the star-spangled skies. When she grew up, she hitched a ride to space as the first Indian-born woman. Today, her journey is an inspiration for thousands of people to reach for the stars.

FUELLED BY CURIOSITY

Born in the small town of Karnal, Haryana, Kalpana took an interest in science and space from an early age. During summers, she often slept in the courtyard, fascinated by the night sky. Interested in flying, she graduated in aeronautical engineering and obtained a doctorate in the subject from the University of Colorado Boulder, USA.

Did you know?

In 2020, a commercial cargo spacecraft bound for the International Space Station *(ISS) was named SS Kalpana Chawla. NASA has even named a hill on Mars after her.*

WE HAVE LIFT OFF!

In 1991, on a lark, Kalpana applied for the NASA Astronauts Corps and got selected. She undertook her first space mission on 19 November 1997 aboard Space Shuttle *Columbia* flight STS-87. With this, she became the first woman of Indian origin to go to space.

CHILD-LIKE FASCINATION

Kalpana always scrambled for a seat near the window of the shuttle, from where she could witness the sunrises and sunsets. Her presence in space reminded her of the fragility of our planet and the need for its conservation. She would get so engrossed in the wonders of space that during mealtimes, she would often miss her mouth and the food would float around her in zero gravity.

Crew members of STS-107

FATAL DISASTER

On 16 January 2003, Kalpana made her second trip to space, aboard Space Shuttle *Columbia* as part of the STS-107 mission. The team performed 80 experiments on subjects, including gene transfer in seeds, study of dust in the Earth's ozone layer, and astronaut health and safety. But while on its way back to the Earth, a few minutes before touchdown, *Columbia* burst into flames and disintegrated. Kalpana and her team perished in a tragic end.

Views in space

In the last couple of years, space missions have sent back some spectacular images of what lies beyond. From the weather conditions on Jupiter to Martian surface, these images help scientists look deeper in the unknown world.

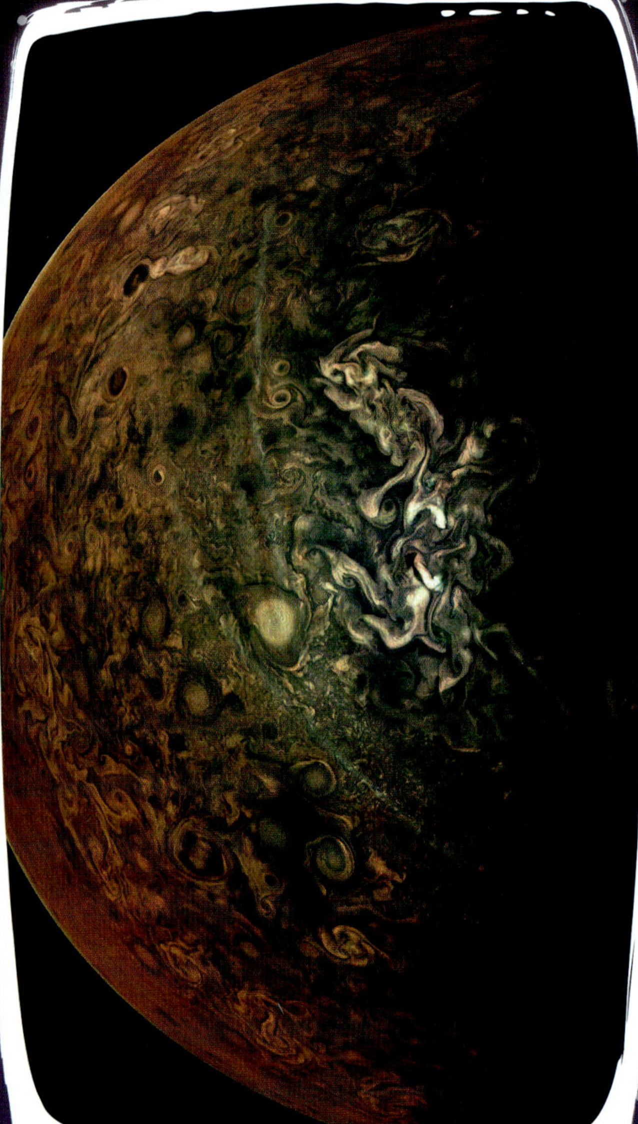

Hazes on Jupiter's northern region

Jupiter's Great Red Spot, captured by *Juno* spacecraft

BepiColombo's views of Mercury

Asteroid Bennu ejecting particles

A close view of Jupiter's moon Ganymede

Discovery of a magnetar by Chandra X-ray Observatory

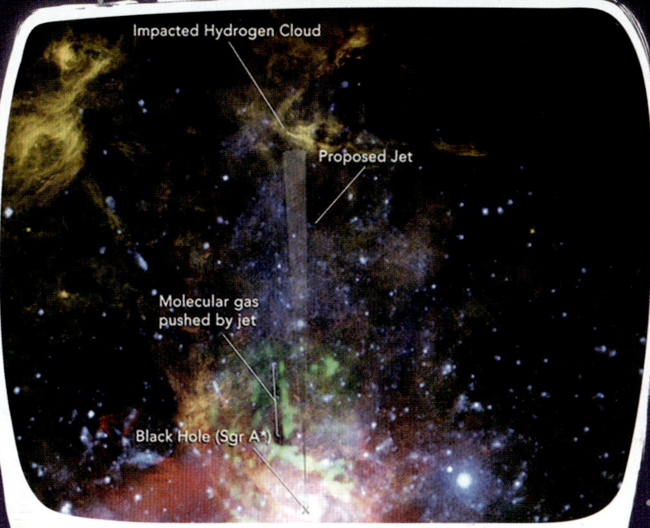

Jets near the Galactic Centre

Panoramic view of a Martian day, taken by *Curiosity* rover

The India connection

In recent years, the world has witnessed many people of Indian origin who have made significant contributions in the field of space exploration and research. The stories of these brilliant minds offer inspiration to people the world over.

SUNITA WILLIAMS

A NASA astronaut, Williams has been a part of two missions to the *International Space Station* (*ISS*) and has set a record for the longest spaceflight by a woman. Her upcoming adventure entails commanding the *Boeing CST-100 Starliner* capsule, which is part of the project to introduce private space taxis.

ASHWIN VASAVADA

What do the missions *Galileo* to Jupiter, *Cassini* to Saturn, *Mars Polar Lander*, and *Mars Odyssey* have in common? Trailblazing scientist Vasavada has worked on all of them. Employed at NASA's Jet Propulsion Laboratory, he oversees the *Curiosity* Mars Rover mission.

SHARMILA BHATTACHARYA

Neurobiologist Bhattacharya focuses on space biosciences, specifically fruit flies and yeast. Her work at the NASA Ames Research Center involves experiments on fruit flies and yeast to test the effects of altered gravity on living organisms' biological systems.

KAMLESH LULLA

In his three decade-long career at NASA, scientist Lulla has trained several astronaut crews, worked on Earth observations and remote sensing in various space programmes, and developed technologies for human exploration of the Moon's surface.

ANITA SENGUPTA

An aerospace engineer and pilot, Sengupta developed the parachute system that helped NASA's *Curiosity* spacecraft land safely on Mars in 2012. She also led NASA's Cold Atom Laboratory project, a facility aboard the *ISS* to study atoms in microgravity and that marks the coldest known spot in the universe.

MADHULIKA GUHATHAKURTA

An astrophysicist, Guhathakurta oversees NASA's Living with a Star programme, which investigates the effects of solar radiations on us and on elements in outer space. She was also instrumental in the *Parker Solar Probe* that ventured millions of kilometres to "touch" the Sun and study it.

SURESH B KULKARNI

Popularly known as the "Rocket Man", Kulkarni has successfully launched 55 rockets under NASA's Space Shuttle programme. He has worked on many important projects, such as the Venus-bound *Magellan*, the Jupiter-bound *Galileo*, the Hubble Space Telescope, and the Shuttle–Mir programme.

RAJA JON VURPUTOOR CHARI

Previously a test pilot in the US Air Force, Raja Chari was the first to graduate from NASA's Artemis programme, making him eligible for future missions to the Moon. He recently commandeered a SpaceX mission to the *ISS*.

Indian Astronomical Observatory

Today, many gigantic telescopes, each housed in its own building, are dotted across the planet's mountain-tops. Mostly, they are the mainstay of an observatory. The Indian Astronomical Observatory (IAO) in the remote Hanle Valley of Ladakh is home to one of the world's highest-located telescopes.

Fact File

Telescope type Optical/infrared and gamma-ray
Location Hanle Valley in Leh district, Ladakh
Operational 2001
Organization Indian Institute of Astrophysics (IIA)

FAR FROM CIVILIZATION, CLOSE TO THE STARS

Dry, cold, and desert-like locations are ideal for space observation. No wonder then that the IAO stands perched atop Mount Saraswati in the western Himalayas, at a staggering height of 4,500 m (14,000 ft) above sea level. The region features low atmospheric water vapour and cloudless skies on most nights, apart from being unaffected by monsoon and snow. It offers a crystal clear glimpse into space.

The HAGAR group of telescopes are used to detect gamma rays from outside the Earth's atmosphere. Seen here is unit 1 of the group.

The Himalayan Chandra Telescope is used to observe exoplanets, comets, and asteroids as well as transients, such as a supernova.

LOOKING THROUGH THE NIGHT

One of IAO's main components is the optical infrared Himalayan Chandra Telescope, which is remotely controlled by the Indian Institute of Astrophysics (IIA) from Hosakote in Karnataka via a satellite link. Also located in the observatory are the HAGAR set of telescopes and the MACE, which is the world's highest-located gamma-ray telescope.

Taking over the Moon

Several countries have attempted to reach the Moon to map its surface, trace its origin, or understand it more closely. So far, India has launched two lunar missions, in 2008 and 2019. Both are named *Chandrayaan*, which means "Moon Vehicle" in Sanskrit.

Chandrayaan-1

India's first mission to the Moon, *Chandrayaan-1*, demonstrated its capability for planetary exploration. The mission included an orbiter and an impactor. The spacecraft was launched on PSLV-C11 on 22 October 2008 and went into lunar orbit on 8 November 2008 to perform more than 3,400 orbits. The main goals of the mission were to create a 3-D map of both the near and far side of the Moon as well as to conduct chemical and mineralogical mapping of the entire lunar surface.

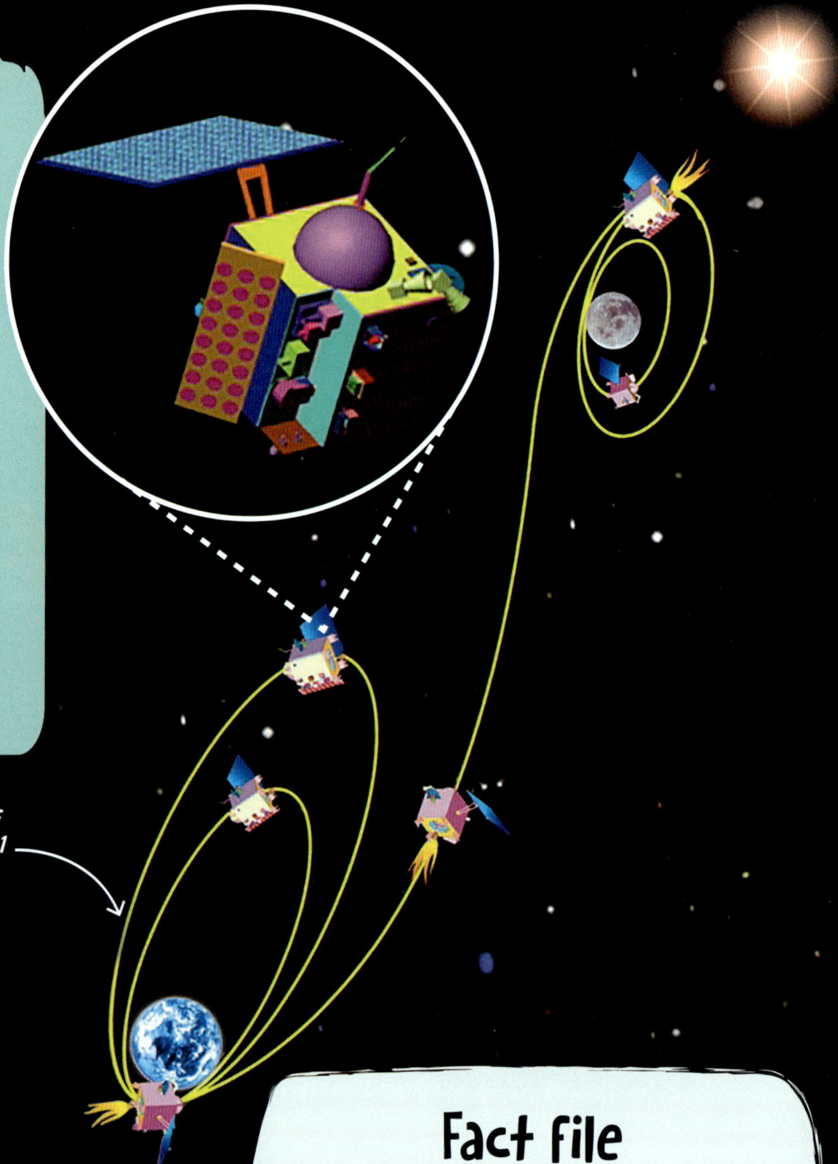

NOT BONE-DRY

The Moon Impact Probe (IMP) was a star feature of this probe. It detached from the *Chandrayaan* and deliberately struck the lunar south pole. The debris from its impact aided the search for water molecules in the thin lunar atmosphere. It was NASA's infrared spectrometer that confirmed the presence of water ice in the polar craters based on how the surface absorbed infrared light. The mission concluded on 29 August 2009.

Fact File

Type of mission Remote sensing and planetary observation

Launch weight 1,380 kg (3,042 lb)

Launch date 22 October 2008

Launch site SDSC, Sriharikota

Launch vehicle PSLV-C11

Total payloads 11

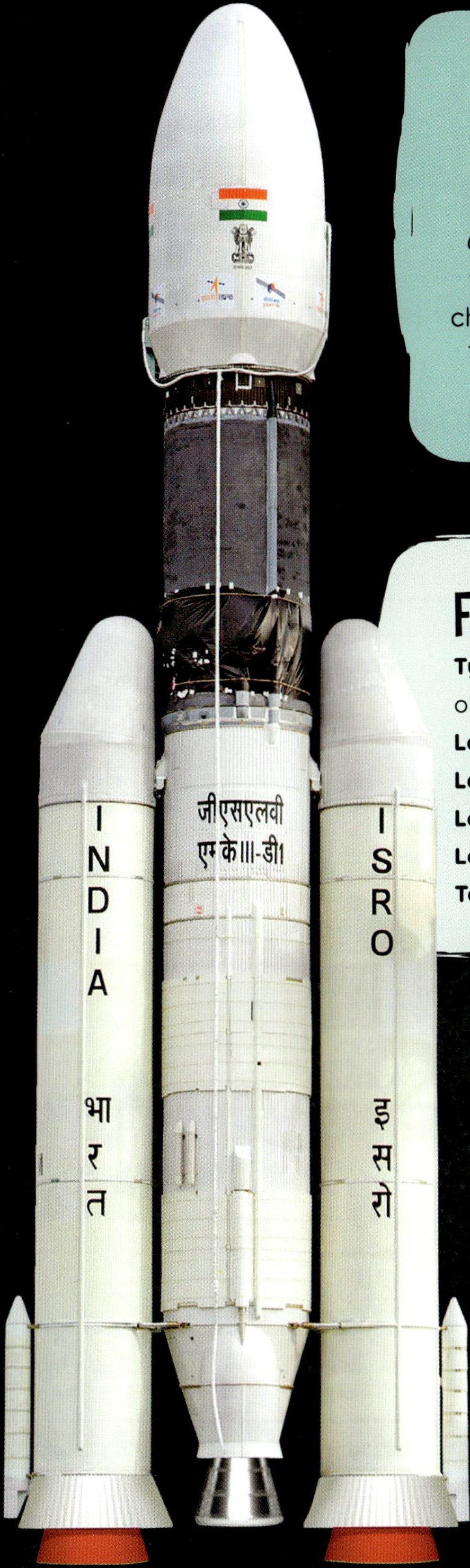

GSLV-MK III launched the *Chandrayaan-2* spacecraft

Chandrayaan-2

Although *Chandrayaan-2* was India's second lunar mission, it had more ambitious objectives – to perform a soft-landing and deploy a rover on the south polar region of the Moon. *Chandrayaan-2* was tasked with collecting information about the surface, mineral identification, and analysing the surface chemical composition and characteristics of the Moon's top soil. The craft was made up of three elements – the lander named *Vikram*, the rover named *Pragyan*, and an improved orbiter.

Fact File

Type of mission Planetary observation and lander
Launch weight 3,850 kg (8,488 lb)
Launch date 22 July 2019
Launch site SDSC, Sriharikota
Launch vehicle GSLV-Mk III - M1
Total payloads 13

WHY EXPLORE THE SOUTH POLE OF THE MOON?

Due to the spherical nature of the Moon, the polar south remains largely in shadow and is thus relatively cooler than the other regions on the Moon. This raises the possibility that water ice may be present in lunar craters near the pole. In 2018, US scientists detected direct evidence for water ice near the lunar poles, using data from a NASA instrument named M3 aboard *Chandrayaan-1*.

THE VIKRAM LANDER

The spacecraft successfully entered orbit on 20 August 2019. About two weeks later, on 6 September, the lander, carrying the rover and five payloads, disengaged from the orbiter and initiated its descent. However, just a short distance away from the surface, the lander crashed on the Moon. But the orbiter has been performing steadily.

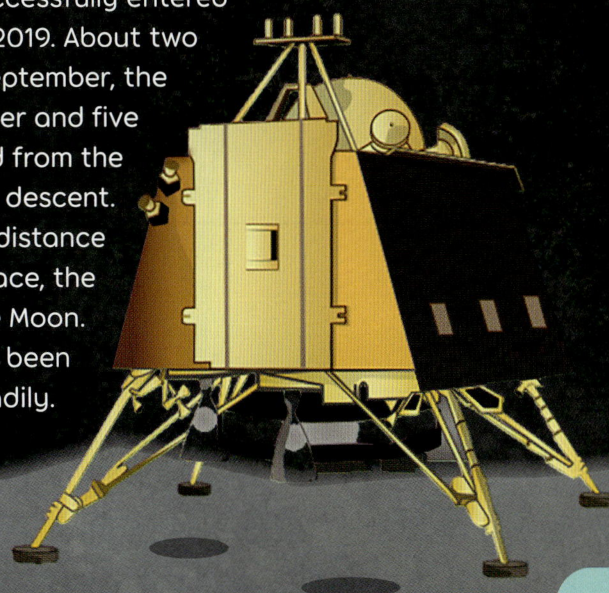

Interplanetary spaceflight

Over the years, many missions have gone to space. They have landed people on the Moon and rovers on Mars. They have peered closely at the planets and even the asteroids, revealing information about their surface and atmosphere.

An artist's impression of *SOHO* spacecraft

SUN

Most spacecraft designed to observe the Sun are not meant to fly close to it. They either stay in the Earth's orbit or venture a little closer to it than the Earth.

SOHO Launched in 1995 by NASA, it has sent back spectacular images of the Sun and has also discovered more than 4,000 comets.

PARKER SOLAR PROBE Launched by NASA in 2018, it became the closest artificial object to go near the Sun.

MOON

In 1959, Soviet missions *Luna 2* and *Luna 3* were the first missions to explore the Moon. Multiple missions have followed since.

APOLLO 11 In 1969, Neil Armstrong and Buzz Aldrin became the first people to walk on the Moon.

CHANDRAYAAN 1 Launched in October 2008, ISRO's *Chandrayaan-1* explored the Moon until 2009.

Chandrayaan-1

MESSENGER spacecraft

MERCURY

Its proximity to the Sun and unstable orbits makes it difficult for a craft to approach it. Thus, it remains the least explored rocky planet.

MARINER 10 Launched in 1973, it was the first craft sent to study the planet and performed three flybys.

MESSENGER A 2011-orbital probe by NASA, it achieved 100 per cent mapping of the planet and collected surface data.

An artist's rendition of *Dawn*

ASTEROID BELT

There are millions of known asteroids, yet only a few have been explored.

DAWN Blasted off in 2007, it examined the two most massive asteroids – Ceres and Vesta.

HAYABUSA This Japanese probe surveyed the Itokawa asteroid and brought back 1,500 particles of asteroid dust.

An artist's concept *Mars Global Surveyor*

VENUS

After the first spacecraft to Venus in the early 1960s, there have been more than 40 missions to it.

VENERA These probes were the first to make a soft landing, send surface images, and record sounds on another planet.

VENUS EXPRESS This mission by ESA has discovered past oceans and confirmed the presence of lightning on the planet.

Venera 15

MARS

The early missions to Mars had little or no success. But the 21st-century missions have performed extremely well.

MARS GLOBAL SURVEYOR Launched in 1996 by NASA, it discovered many long gorges, believed to be carved by running water in the past.

CURIOSITY This rover landed on Mars in 2012 to explore the planet's surface. It also took the first-ever selfie on another planet.

SATURN

This planet has been visited by many probes since the 1970s, although the initial probes were all flybys.

VOYAGER The twin *Voyager* spacecraft presented detailed views of Saturn's moons.

CASSINI In the course of 20 years in space, this mission has showed us the complexity of Saturn's rings and the dramatic processes within them.

Model of *Voyager*

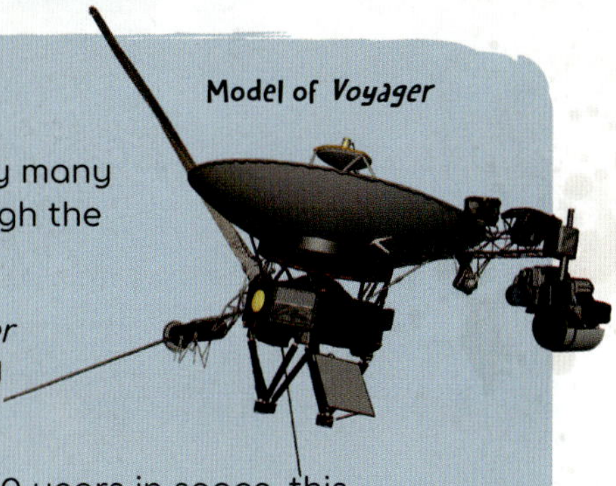

URANUS AND NEPTUNE

Distant Uranus and Neptune have been explored through telescopes and by a lone probe so far. But future missions have been proposed.

VOYAGER 2 Launched in 1986 by NASA, this spacecraft discovered two new rings of Uranus and revealed that winds on Neptune were the strongest in our solar system.

JUPITER

The most visited outer planet, its exploration began in the 1970s and continues into the 21st century.

PIONEER 10 It clicked the first-ever close-up shots of the planet and its Galilean moon, and detected its magnetic field

GALILEO It was the first to orbit around the planet and witnessed the impact of Comet Shoemaker–Levy 9.

An artist's concept of *Galileo*

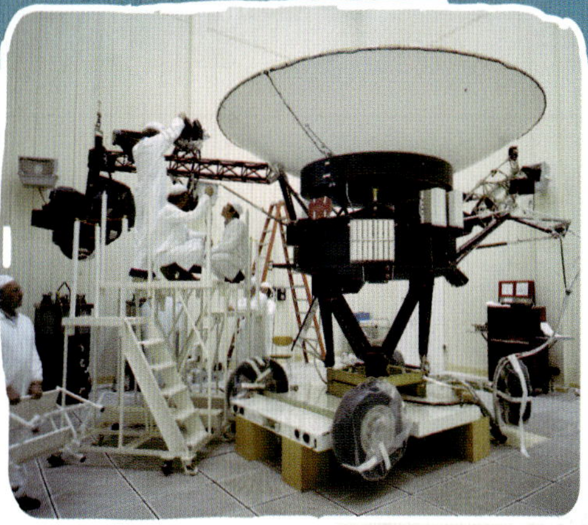

Voyager 2 being tested

Megha-Tropiques

In 2011, ISRO and the French space agency, Centre National D'Etudes Spatiales (CNES), deployed a joint satellite mission into orbit for climate research. Called *Megha-Tropiques*, its main objective is to study the water cycle in the tropical atmosphere.

WHAT'S IT DOING UP THERE?

Focusing on the Earth's tropical region between the 10° and 20° latitudes, *Megha-Tropiques* studies the water cycle and energetic exchanges, and reports on cloud clusters, monsoon systems, cyclones, and other weather phenomena.

Deployed *Megha-Tropiques* spacecraft at ISRO

Equipped with both day- and night-viewing capabilities, it passes over the Indian subcontinent about a dozen times in a day and relays real-time information about the weather conditions to scientists. This is especially useful for an agrarian country like India, which is heavily dependent on the monsoon for its agricultural sector to flourish. In the long run, *Megha-Tropiques*'s observations will be useful in studying global climate change.

Fun Fact

Megha literally means "cloud" in Sanskrit while tropiques is the French word for "tropics".

WHAT INSTRUMENTS DOES IT CARRY?

There are four payloads, or instruments for conducting scientific experiments, that are carried by *Megha-Tropiques*.

MADRAS for capturing microwave images.

ROSA for measuring humidity and temperature profiles.

SCARAB for measuring the radiations entering, reflected, absorbed, and emitted by the Earth as well as evaporation, condensation, and precipitation.

SAPHIR for measuring and analysing humidity in the atmosphere.

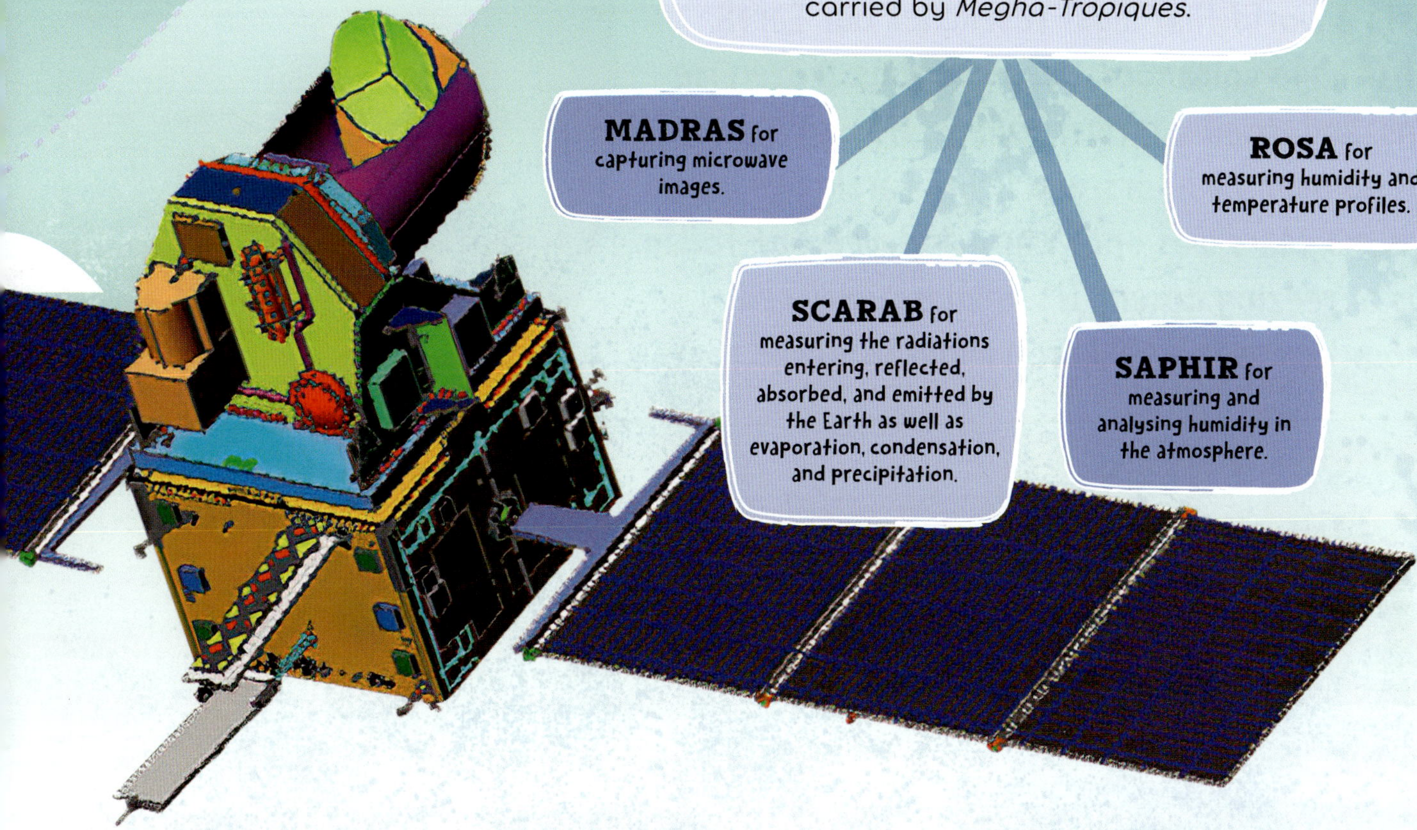

TRISHNA (Thermal infraRed Imaging Satellite for High resolution Natural resource Assessment) satellite

WHAT HAPPENED NEXT?

Soon after the launch of *Megha-Tropiques*, France and India got together again in 2013 to launch *SARAL-AltiKa*, a satellite mission for studying ocean circulation and sea surface elevation. In 2021, plans for a third joint mission, *TRISHNA*, were announced. It is geared towards monitoring the water systems in the Earth's ecosystems through thermal mapping.

Fact file

Weight 1,000 kg (2,205 lb)

Cost Rs 500 crores

Launch date 12 October 2011

Launch site Sriharikota Range, Andhra Pradesh

Mars

The fourth planet in the solar system, Mars hosts a world that most resembles our Earth. It has huge volcanoes, deep canyons, frozen ice caps, and dried-up river valleys. Its day is only a little over 24 hours, and it has Earth-like seasons. Mars was once warm and wet, but today, it is a freezing desert. Its unique rusty-red colour comes from the iron minerals in the rocks.

FROSTY POLES

Mars has ice caps at both poles. They are mainly made of water ice with some frozen carbon dioxide, known as dry ice. In summer, when the poles are exposed to sunlight, the dry ice evaporates and shrinks the size of the caps. They again grow back in winter when the temperature drops.

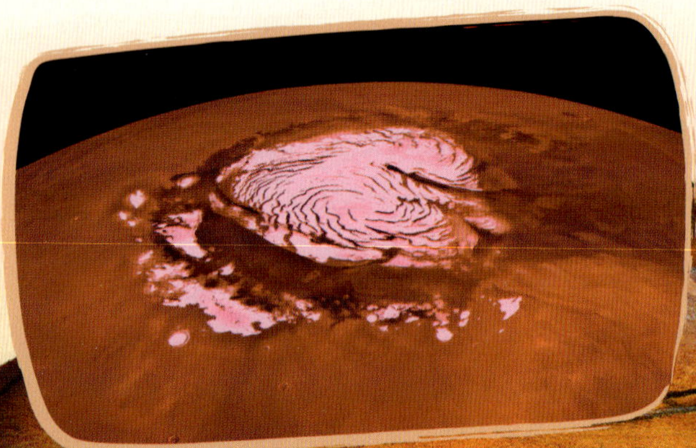

WHERE IS THE WATER?

Today, Mars is freezing cold and its thin atmosphere can't support liquid water on its surface. However, dry crater lakes and winding channels suggest that water flowed on Martian surface long ago, which gradually escaped into space due to the planet's smaller size and weaker gravity.

1964 *Mariner 4* makes the first flyby, taking 21 images.

1969 *Mariner 7* successfully returns 126 images.

1971 *Mariner 9* orbits Mars successfully, becoming the first spacecraft to orbit another planet.

1976 *Viking 1* makes the first landing on Martian surface.

1996 *Mars Global Surveyor* is launched to map the whole surface of Mars.

1997 *Mars Pathfinder* delivers the first successful rover.

Fun Fact

Mars has two small, potato-shaped moons called Phobos and Deimos. They may have been asteroids that were pulled into orbit around Mars by its gravity. Phobos is slightly larger than Deimos and is much closer to Mars. Both are heavily cratered and are covered in a thick layer of dust.

DESTINATION MARS

With more than 40 spacecraft and rovers visiting it so far, Mars is now the most explored planet in the solar system. As of 2021, three rovers – *Curiosity*, *Perseverance*, and *Zhurong* – are roaming on the Martian surface, conducting on-the-spot investigations. However, visiting Mars in person is still a dream of many astronauts, and future missions may attempt that as well.

NASA's *Curiosity* rover takes a selfie using a camera on its long robotic arm.

2003 *Mars Express* orbiter begins taking detailed pictures of the planet.

2008 *Phoenix* lands in Martian Arctic and operates for more than five months, before its batteries die out.

2012 NASA's *Curiosity* rover lands on Mars and begins exploring the surface.

2016 *ExoMars Trace Gas Orbiter* is launched by Europe and Russia to study gases in the Martian atmosphere.

2021 *Ingenuity*, a robotic helicopter, achieves the first powered flight on Mars.

Mangalyaan

No country got its Mars mission right on the first try, except India, in 2014. That's when the *Mars Orbiter Mission* (*MOM*) or *Mangalyaan* went into orbit around Mars, making India the first Asian nation to reach the planet's orbit. Equipped with hi-tech instruments, the mission set out to study the Martian atmosphere, and even look for signs of life.

Mars Orbiter Mission spacecraft sitting atop a rocket before launch

HOW TO BUILD A LOW-COST MARTIAN ORBITER

Stick to a short time period It took only 15 months to develop and build the *Mangalyaan* spacecraft.

Use lightweight materials During lift-off, the orbiter weighed only 1,337 kg (2,948 lb). It meant less consumption of fuel.

Make only one model To reduce costs, only one model was built and ISRO relied heavily on software for testing.

Use homemade technologies Priority was given to keep the design as simple as possible, and use India-made materials.

ON TO MARS!

On 5 November 2013, *Mangalyaan* blasted off aboard a PSLV C-25 rocket and began orbiting the Earth. To cover such long distance with the least amount of fuel, scientists at ISRO gradually put the spacecraft into higher and higher orbits around the Earth, waiting for Mars to reach its closest distance to the Earth. Finally after about a month, like a perfectly timed slingshot, the spacecraft was hurled away from the Earth orbit on a spectacular cruise to Mars. A nail-biting, 10 month-long journey ensued, before it reached the Martian orbit on 24 September 2014.

Fun Fact

The Mars Orbiter Mission cost less than the Hollywood film Gravity, making it the cheapest interplanetary mission ever.

ALL THIS FOR WHAT?

Mangalyaan carried five payloads or instruments to conduct a variety of experiments.

METHANE SENSOR FOR MARS (MSM) To measure methane in the Martian atmosphere. Unfortunately, the device wasn't sensitive enough to be able to detect any trace of methane.

THERMAL INFRARED IMAGING SPECTROMETER (TIS) To map surface composition and study the minerals on Mars. It provided some clear infrared (thermal) maps of the planet.

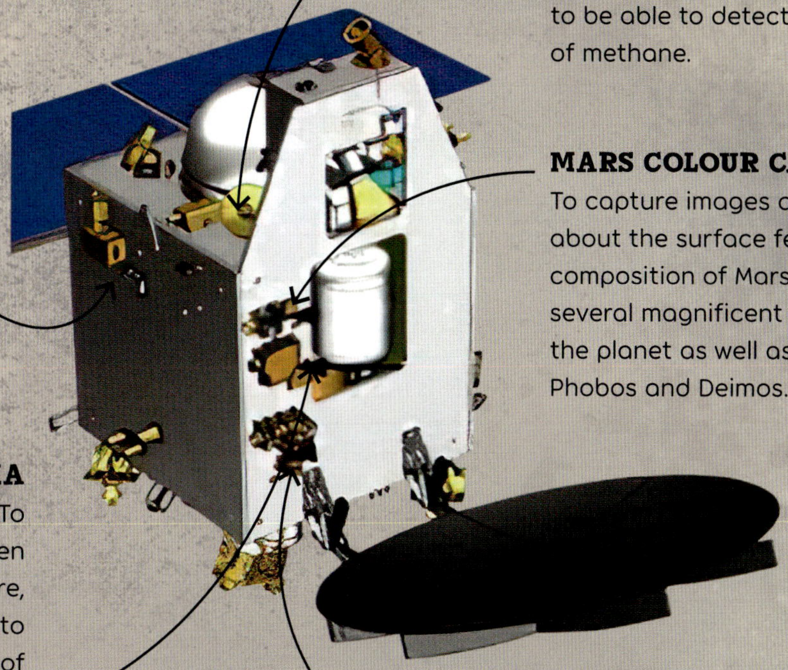

MARS COLOUR CAMERA (MCC) To capture images and gather data about the surface features and composition of Mars. It captured several magnificent images of the planet as well as its moons – Phobos and Deimos.

LYMAN ALPHA PHOTOMETER (LAP) To measure the amount of hydrogen and deuterium in the atmosphere, which would allow us to understand the loss of water from the planet.

MARS EXOSPHERIC NEUTRAL COMPOSITION ANALYSER (MENCA) To study the uppermost region of the planet's atmosphere.

Fact file

Type of satellite Science and exploration
Launch weight 1,337 kg (2,948 lb)
Estimated cost Rs 450 crores
Launch date 5 November 2013
Launch site Sriharikota, Andhra Pradesh, India
In orbit More than six years

Women behind Mangalyaan

The *Mars Orbiter Mission* (MOM), popularly known as the *Mangalyaan* mission, was a momentous occasion that marked India's successful maiden attempt at Mars. A group of trailblazing women stood at the forefront of this herculean project and made headlines for their work.

"It is like the human brain. It receives signals from sensors like your eyes, ears, nerve endings. If there is a problem anywhere in your body, your brain reacts immediately. That is what we had to build for the orbiter in 10 months from scratch."

In an interview with WIRED, 2017

"The main challenge was to make them very compact, lightweight and low-power, because the mission was to be launched with minimum fuel. We fought for every gram."

In an interview with GQ India, 2019

RITU KARIDHAL

DEPUTY OPERATIONS DIRECTOR

A postgraduate in physics, Karidhal has led several ISRO missions and received the ISRO Young Scientist Award in 2007. For the Mars mission, her team was responsible for the design and development of a self-autonomous software system, which made it possible for the orbiter to monitor and control its functions independently in space.

MOUMITA DUTTA

PROJECT MANAGER

A physicist, Dutta played a significant role in developing one of the five payloads of the *Mars Orbiter Mission* – the methane sensor payload. It looks for signatures of methane in the Martian atmosphere as methane may indicate the presence of microbial life. She also developed a colour camera to help capture Mars' surface and composition.

Did you know?

Women held 27 per cent of the key positions in the mission.

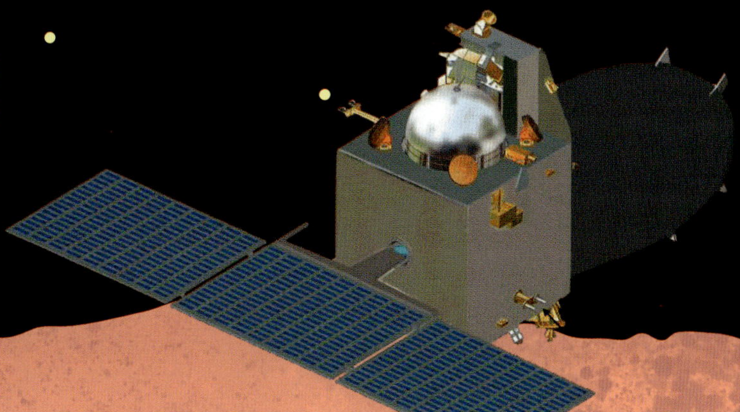

Mars Orbiter Mission spacecraft

"It was very important for India, not just for ISRO. It has put us on a different pedestal, foreign countries are looking at us for collaborations and the importance and attention we got was justified."

In an interview with BBC, 2016

"In space, no mistake is acceptable. We call it zero defect."

In an interview with Medium, 2017

NANDINI HARINATH

PROJECT MANAGER AND MISSION DESIGN AND DEPUTY OPERATIONS DIRECTOR

Harinath's liking for mathematics and physics propelled her into a career with ISRO. For *Mangalyaan*, she helped calculate and design the predetermined path that the capsule should take to reach the Red Planet. If it suddenly changed its direction, her team had the means to steer it back on the track.

MINAL ROHIT

PROJECT MANAGER AND SYSTEM ENGINEER FOR METHANE SENSORS

Minal started her career at ISRO by working on providing medical and education access to rural parts of India via ISRO's communication satellites. For *Mangalyaan*, her team was responsible for incorporating the components of the payloads to work together in harmony. Minal painstakingly designed the plans and procedures to integrate the subsystems of the methane sensor into a scientific instrument.

Saraswati Supercluster

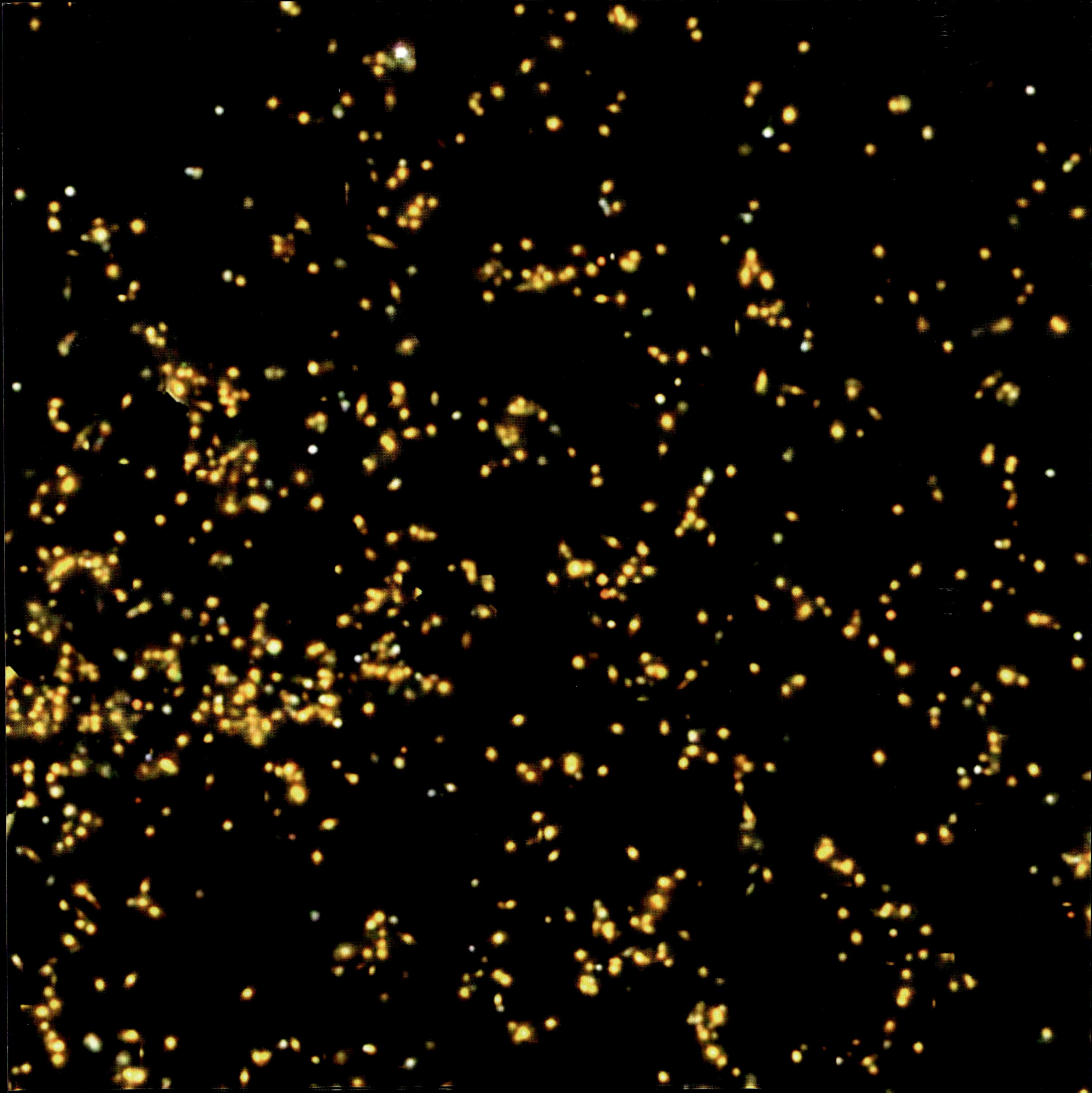

In 2017, a team of Indian astrophysicists from IUCAA and IISER in Pune, NIT in Jamshedpur, and Newman College in Thodupuzha discovered a massive supercluster. The structure, resembling a colossal wall of galaxies, was located an astonishing 4 billion light years away, in the direction of the constellation Pisces. Named after the Hindu goddess Saraswati, this supercluster is believed to be more than 10 billion years old and stretches across a distance of 600 million light years. This makes it one of the largest superclusters to be discovered and also the furthest.

AstroSat

For many centuries, astronomers had access to only one instrument to observe the sky – the human eye. Then, the invention of the telescope in the early 17th century revolutionized observational astronomy. In the quest to dive deeper into space, humans built larger and more advanced telescopes, stationed on the Earth. The next step was to observe space from space.

Fact file

Satellite type Science and exploration
Weight 1,515 kg
Launch date 28 September 2015
Launch site Satish Dhawan Space Centre (SDSC), Sriharikota, Andhra Pradesh
In orbit For more than 5 years

INDIGENOUS SATELLITE

The launch of AstroSat, India's first multi-wavelength astronomy mission, marked the country's departure from reliance on international resources for X-ray and ultraviolet (UV) data. India became a part of the small group of countries that have a space-borne observatory. Its cuboid-shaped satellite has five payloads, four of which can observe the same part of the sky simultaneously. It gives astronomers a unique opportunity to study celestial objects in various rays, such as UV and gamma, at once.

DISCOVERIES AND EXPLORATIONS

AstroSat has most famously detected UV radiation from the AUDFs01 galaxy, which is located 9.3 billion light years away. In the five years of its operation, it has carried out more than 1,100 observations of 800 unique celestial sources. These include stars, star clusters, small and large satellite galaxies of the Milky Way, supernovae, coronal explosion, and active galactic nuclei.

An image of Wolf-Lundmark-Melott, a dwarf galaxy 3 million light years away, as seen from the Ultra Violet Imaging Telescope on board the AstroSat.

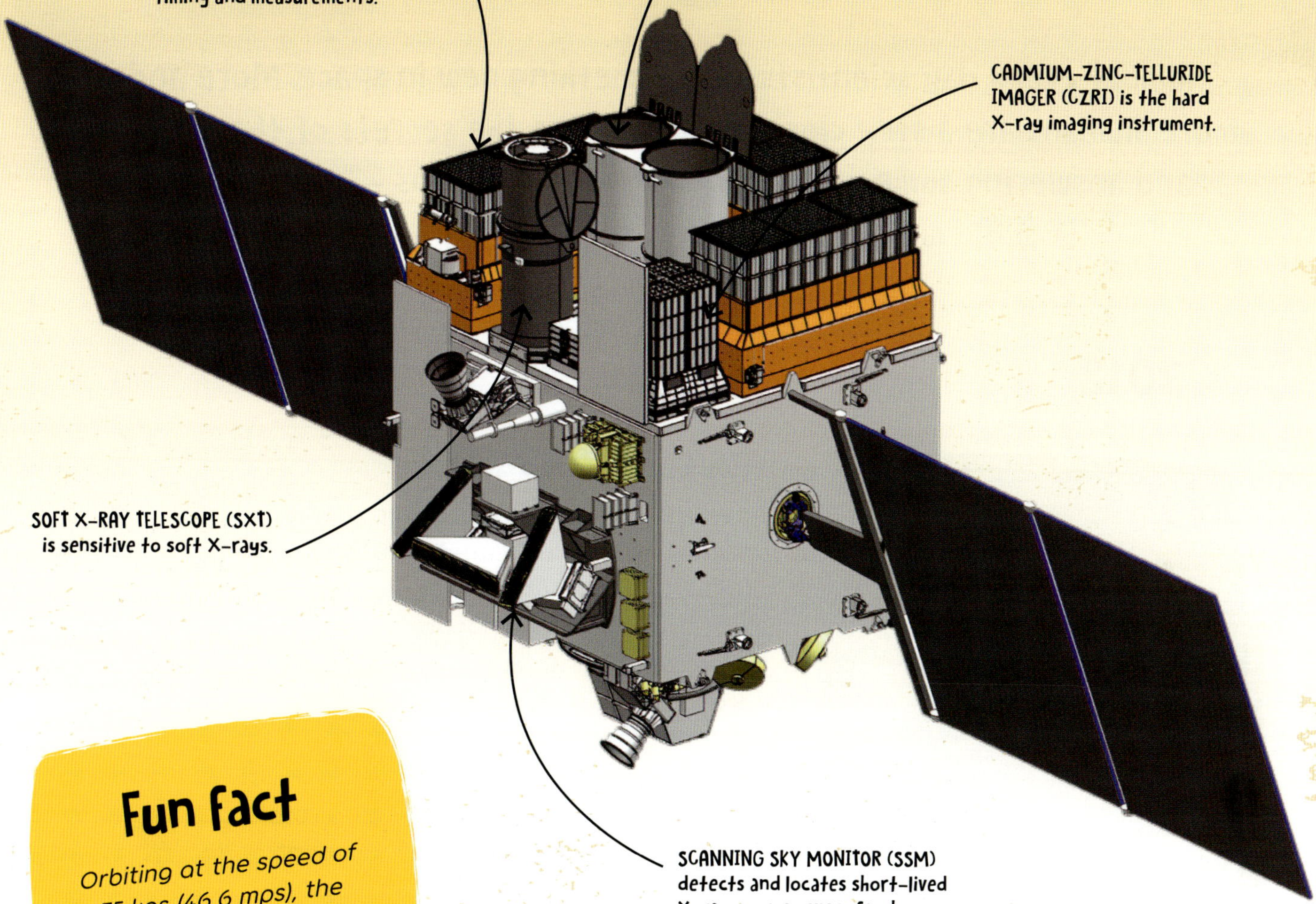

Fun fact

Orbiting at the speed of 75 kps (46.6 mps), the AstroSat is almost 200 times faster than the Shatabdi Express, considered one of the fastest trains in India.

What are space telescopes?

Celestial objects emit various rays, including X-rays and ultraviolet rays, which cannot penetrate the Earth's atmosphere. But, these can be perceived by telescopes in space. Unlike observatories on land, space telescopes are not affected by temperature, clouds, weather, blurring, or light pollution of a nearby city. NASA's Hubble Space Telescope is the most well-known in the world.

Breakthrough discoveries

Almost every day scientists find something new in space. More and more, humans are a step closer to unpacking the secrets of the universe and answering some of the fundamental questions – "who are we?", "how did we get here?", and "what are we doing here?"

2012

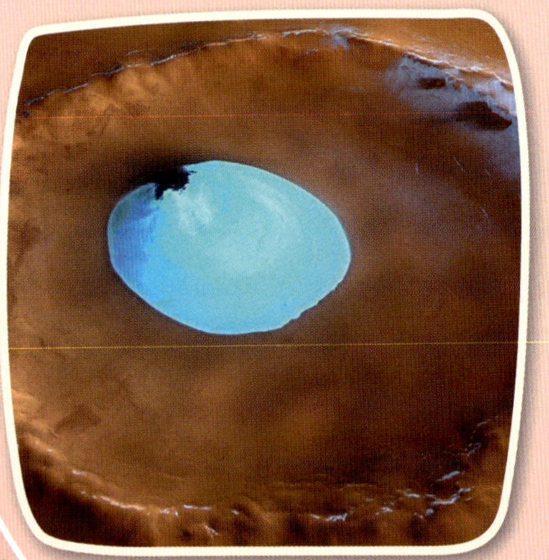

WATER ON MARS

Scientists always suspected the presence of water on the Red Planet. NASA's *Curiosity* rover sent the first physical proof to confirm this. Rounded pebbles and gravel, characteristic of a riverbed, were found near the Gale Crater. Turns out that the Martian surface wasn't always a bone-dry expanse. For millions of years, fast-flowing water gushed across its surface, leaving behind a network of deep canyons as it snaked through.

2016

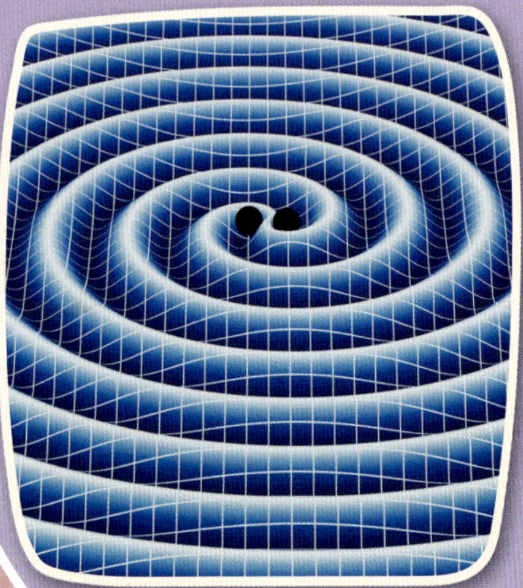

GRAVITATIONAL WAVES

In 1916, German-born physicist Albert Einstein predicted the existence of gravitational waves that could be described as feeble ripples in the fabric of space–time. A century later, sophisticated detectors in the USA picked up evidence to support his claim. About 1.3 billion years ago, two massive black holes smashed into each other and merged into one. So powerful was the collision that it sent a shudder through the universe. In 2016, the ripples washed past the Earth, making their presence known.

2016

PROXIMA CENTAURI B

About 4.25 light-years away from the Sun lies the dwarf star Proxima Centauri. Scientists have found an exoplanet, which they have named Proxima Centauri b, orbiting it. The planet is located in the Goldilocks Zone, which means it has just the right temperature to sustain liquid water. It receives as much solar energy from its star as the Earth receives from the Sun. It has all the right conditions to support life.

2017

NEUTRON STAR COLLISION

A neutron star is formed in the mega explosion that follows the death of a massive star. For the first time ever, scientists captured a pulse of gravitational waves emanating from the collision of two neutron stars that occurred 130 million years ago. It was revealed that the powerful impact generated plumes of heavy metals, including gold, silver, and platinum, in quantities large enough to fill all the Earth's oceans.

Black hole

One of the most powerful and extreme things in the universe, black holes are wildly weird and complicated. They aren't actual holes, but a spherical region of very strong gravity. They are formed when stars much more massive than the Sun explode as supernova and collapse under their own gravity.

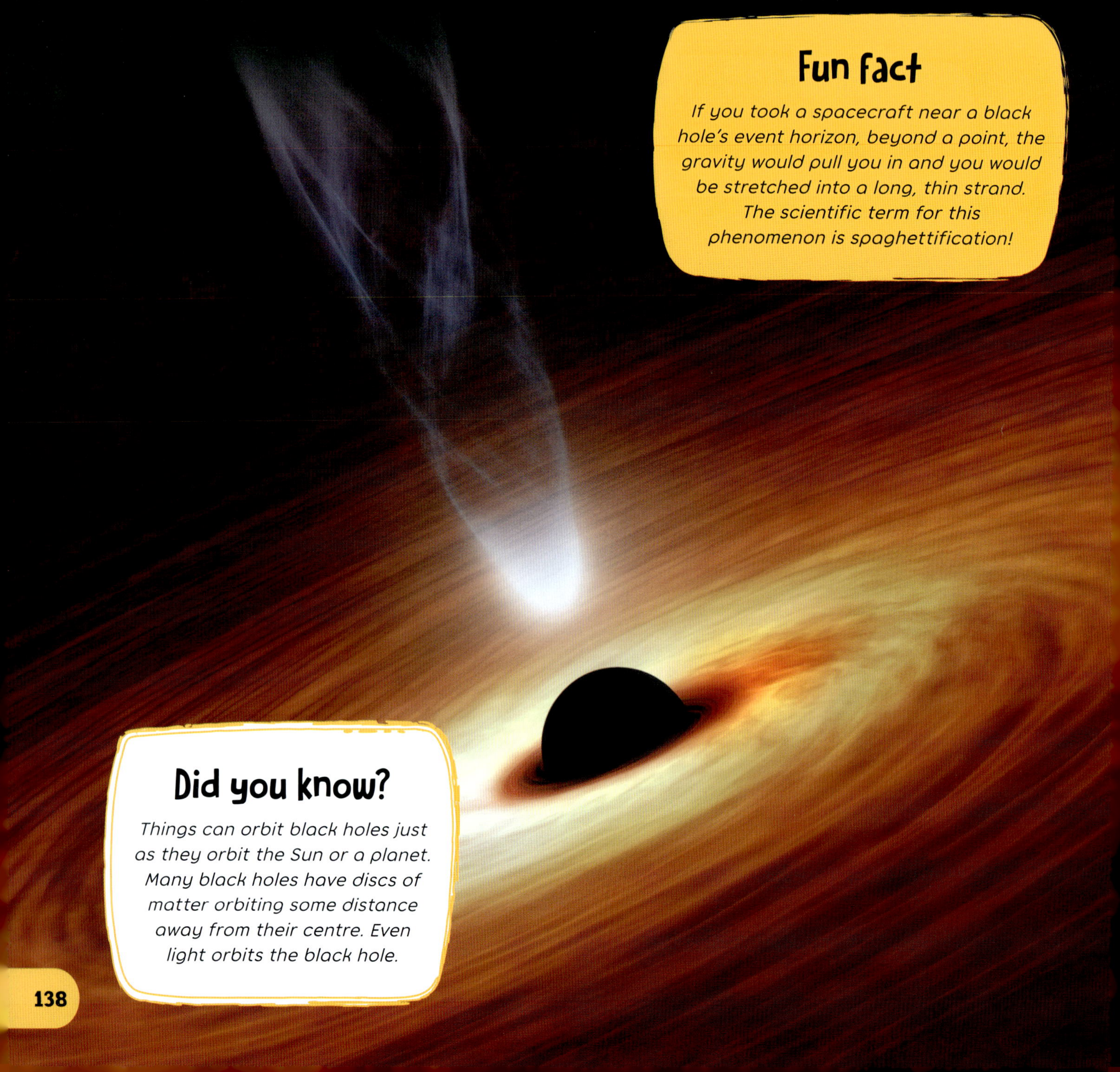

Fun fact

If you took a spacecraft near a black hole's event horizon, beyond a point, the gravity would pull you in and you would be stretched into a long, thin strand. The scientific term for this phenomenon is spaghettification!

Did you know?

Things can orbit black holes just as they orbit the Sun or a planet. Many black holes have discs of matter orbiting some distance away from their centre. Even light orbits the black hole.

PIONEERS IN BLACK HOLE RESEARCH

EINSTEIN

Almost a century ago, German-born physicist Albert Einstein proposed that the gravitational pull of black holes could be so immense that they can twist magnetic fields and bend light waves right around them, not just trap them. Researchers have now proven his theory to be true.

SUBRAHMANYAN CHANDRASEKHAR

Nobel Laureate and astrophysicist Subrahmanyan Chandrasekhar predicted at what mass a star could or could not collapse into a black hole. This came to be known as Chandrasekhar Limit.

STEPHEN HAWKING

English physicist Stephen Hawking found that black holes could produce radiation. It disproved the belief that nothing can escape a black hole's gravity. On this basis, Hawking theorized that it is possible for a black hole to eventually fade away.

C V VISHVESHWARA

In 2015, the Laser Interferometer Gravitational-Wave Observatory (LIGO) used Indian physicist C V Vishveshwara's calculations in the discovery of gravitational waves.

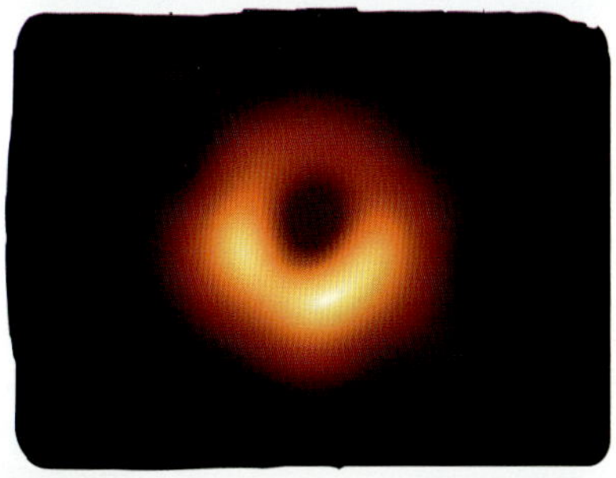

The first black hole image

Although it was known that they existed, black holes were not seen until recently. In 2019, a global network of observatories collected data from about 55 million light years away from the Earth and produced the first computerized image of a black hole.

Going commercial

Space tourism is not a distant dream. Private companies across the world have already started investing in the possibility of quick getaways to space. Now, people can travel to space for a few hours, experience weightlessness, and take in the spectacular view of the Earth. Of course, these trips are still expensive, but as technology develops, costs are expected to fall and more people will be able to afford spaceflight.

WORLD VIEW

American near space exploration and technology company World View plans to take people all the way up to the stratosphere in its gigantic, football stadium-sized balloon satellite, or "Stratollite". The capsule would lift off from one of the seven designated spaceport locations and take passengers to the edge of space, from where they can experience the unrestricted view of the Earth and the darkness of space.

TICKET COST
$125,000

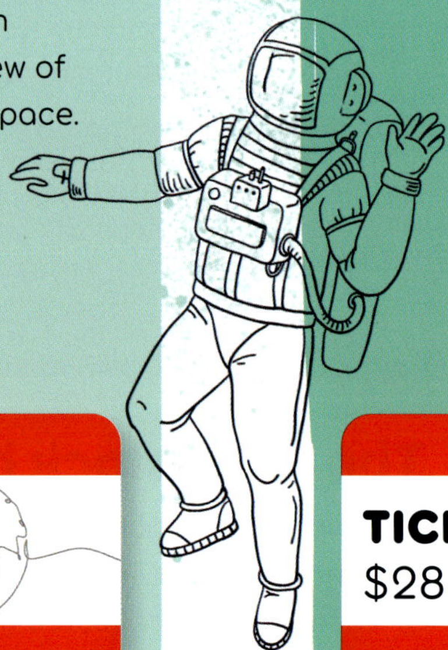

BLUE ORIGIN

American entrepreneur Jeff Bezos' company Blue Origin will take people to space aboard a reusable launch vehicle. Tourists will be able to experience 15 minutes of weightlessness before the capsule parachutes back to the Earth. The company is also working towards relocating factories to space to avoid pollution on the Earth.

TICKET COST
$28 million

Trip to space

On 11 July 2021, aeronautical engineer Sirisha Bandla became the third woman of Indian origin to go to space. She accompanied Virgin Galactic's founder Richard Branson to outer space. Taking off from New Mexico, USA, they flew to the edge of the Earth to a height of 88 km (55 miles). Their mission, called *Unity 22*, served as a test flight for full-fledged commercial flights in the near future.

Richard Branson, Sirisha Bandla (left), and other crew members after their trip to space

VIRGIN GALACTIC

British businessman Richard Branson's spaceflight company Virgin Galactic is another key player in the field of space tourism. Between 2018 and 2019, the company tested some suborbital spaceflights with its spacecraft *Unity*. In 2021, Branson travelled to outer space in a test flight.

TICKET COST
$450,000

SpaceX

American aerospace company SpaceX paved the way for space tourism and continues to revolutionize the industry. It was the first private company to successfully send a crewed mission to orbit and to the *International Space Station* (*ISS*). But the company's ultimate aim is to colonize Mars.

TICKET COST
$55 million

Mission Shakti

For a long time, only USA, Russia, and China possessed anti-satellite weapons. But in 2019, India's ISRO and the Defence Research and Development Organisation (DRDO), in a joint programme, successfully tested an anti-satellite weapon. The operation was code-named Mission Shakti.

WHAT IS ASAT?

Anti-satellite weapon, or ASAT, is used to cripple or destroy satellites in space. It is launched into space with the help of powerful rocket engines. Once it has achieved the desired orbital height, the top portion of the missile, called the Kill Vehicle, collides with the target satellite directly without the use of any explosives. Sometimes, instead of physically destroying the adversary's satellite, ASATs use other modes, such as laser technology, to damage the target.

THE TARGET

For the test mission, India chose an existing Indian satellite in low orbit as a target. ISRO was asked to launch a 740-kg (1,631-lb) "Microsatellite-R" on 24 January 2019 as a regular customer launch. The dimensions of the target satellite were chosen to replicate a typical defence satellite. The target satellite was moving at the speed of about 8 kps (5mps) at the height of about 300 km (186.4 miles). The ASAT was assigned a precision trajectory to intercept and collide with the target satellite.

THE INTERCEPTOR

A missile, designated Prithvi Defence Vehicle Mark-II, was used in Mission Shakti. It was a three-stage interceptor missile with two solid rocket boosters embodying the first two stages, and the Kill Vehicle being the third. It was launched from the APJ Abdul Kalam Island launch complex near Odisha. This missile had the capability to hit satellites up to a height of 1,000 km (621 miles) in space. But the test was done at a lower level in order to ensure that debris from the hit fell back on the Earth and did not pose any risk for other satellites.

SIGNIFICANCE OF THE MISSION

India's space programme has grown rapidly over the last few decades. Apart from missions to the Moon and Mars, there are several Indian satellites orbiting in space. The prime objective of Mission Shakti was to ensure and demonstrate that India has the potential and technology to protect its assets in space.

A stamp, released in 2020, commemorating the launch of India's first anti-satellite missile

India's proposed space station

Only a few countries in the world have independently launched and operated their own space stations. Plans are afoot for India to become the fourth nation to do so. With the help of studies and observations made during the *Gaganyaan* mission, ISRO plans to develop a space station that will weigh 20 tonnes and orbit the Earth at an altitude of 400 km (249 miles). Equipped with life support systems, it will allow astronauts to live on board for 15–20 days at a stretch. This image shows the scale model of the proposed space station.

Looking ahead

Ever since India launched its space programme, it has moved by leaps and bounds in space exploration. The country is constantly aiming to diversify its area of research. ISRO has many exciting missions in the pipeline, involving exploring other planets and even human spaceflight, a first for India.

CHANDRAYAAN-3

The Moon continues to be a subject of fascination for ISRO. *Chandrayaan-3* will attempt a landing on the unexplored lunar south pole. The spacecraft's *Vikram* lander will carry, among other instruments, a thermal probe and a seismometer to study "moonquakes". The *Pragyan* rover will carry spectrometers to investigate the composition of the lunar crust.

ADITYA-L1

In one of the most ambitious undertakings by ISRO, the indigenously built *Aditya-L1* satellite will unravel the mysteries of the Sun. It will make a journey of 1.5 million km (932,057 miles) to reach the Sun's corona. There, it will brave temperatures of more than 5700 °C (10,000 °F) and observe the Sun's atmosphere and magnetic field up close.

GAGANYAAN

Human spaceflight is a realm largely dominated by the USA and Russia. However, ISRO is working hard towards getting its foot in the door via the *Gaganyaan* programme. The first stage comprises two uncrewed test missions. The ultimate mission will follow soon after, in which a crew of two or three Indian astronauts will travel to low Earth orbit (LEO) for a period of seven days.

SHUKRAYAAN

The planet Venus has always been rather neglected with most of the world's attention on Mars. So far, Japanese orbiter *Akatsuki* is the only one studying Venus. ISRO's *Shukrayaan* mission will launch a Venus-bound orbiter to map its surface and conduct several experiments to understand its atmosphere. The launch is scheduled for 2024 and the plan is for the orbiter to study the planet for four years.

Across the world

JAMES WEBB SPACE TELESCOPE

Jointly developed by NASA, the ESA, and the CSA, the James Webb Space Telescope (JWST) was launched in 2021 as the successor to the Hubble Space Telescope. This infrared space observatory is designed to detect infrared radiations from objects within and outside our solar system. Its aim is to provide new information about the early universe, galaxies, and stars.

NASA technicians use a crane to lift the JWST

Glossary

Asteroid A giant piece of rock that orbits the Sun.

Astrolabe A device that is used to measure the angle between objects in the sky and the horizon.

Astronomer A scientist who studies Space and its objects.

Astrophysicist A person who studies the nature of stars and galaxies.

Azimuth The direction of a celestial object from the observer.

Babylonians People who lived in the city of Babylon in southern Mesopotamia.

Brahman A member of the priestly caste in Hinduism.

Comet An object made of ice and dust, which develops a tail as it travels near to the Sun.

Compass A navigation instrument used for identifying direction.

Cosmonaut Russian (or Soviet) equivalent for an astronaut.

Electromagnetic spectrum The complete range of electromagnetic radiation, from gamma rays to radio waves.

Equatorial mount A mount for telescopes that allows movements along two axes, one of which is parallel to Earth's axis.

Event horizon The area around the centre of the black hole where nothing can escape.

Geostationary Earth orbit (GEO) A type of orbit used by satellites to stay in one location above the Earth.

Geosynchronous orbit (GSO) A high Earth orbit that allows satellites to match the Earth's rotation. In this orbit, a satellite will appear to return to the same point in the sky at the same time each day.

Gravity The force of attraction that pulls objects towards each other.

Ionosphere The layer in the upper reaches of the atmosphere where atoms and molecules are ionized by solar radiation.

Kill Vehicle The top portion of a missile, which can manoeuvre itself and collide with the target satellite directly without the use of any explosives.

Latitudes Imaginary lines running horizontally on the Earth.

Longitudes Imaginary lines running north to south on the Earth. They come together at the North and South poles.

Low Earth orbit (LEO) An orbit that is relatively close to the Earth's surface.

Microwave radiometer An instrument that measures thermally-emitted electromagnetic radiation.

Module An individual unit of a spacecraft.

Observatory A place where astronomers study the movements of objects in the sky.

Payloads The cargo carried into Space by a rocket.

Remote sensing Seeing and recording a planet's features from a long distance.

Spectroheliograph An astronomical instrument used to capture a monochromatic image of the Sun.

Spectrum A graph that shows the intensity of light being emitted over a range of energies.

Stone Age The time when the first people lived. During this period, humans used stone tools and survived by hunting and gathering.

Sumerians People who inhabited the southernmost region of Mesopotamia.

Supernova The brilliant, explosive death of a star that sometimes outshines its own galaxy.

Unidentified flying object (UFO) An aerial object of unknown nature that is believed to be from another planet.

Vedas Ancient Hindu texts believed to have been revealed to the sages by gods themselves. They are four in number – *Rigveda*, *Samaveda*, *Yajurveda*, and *Atharvaveda*.

Wavelength The distance between two troughs of a wave.

Index

R

S

T

U

V

W

Y

Z

Acknowledgments

The publisher would like to thank: Nayan Keshan, Arushi Mathur, and Kanika Praharaj for research and ideation, Hina Jain for assistance with content planning, Kathakali Banerjee for editorial assistance, Deepak Negi and Vagisha Pushp for picture research, Bharti Karakoti and Stuti Tiwari for design assistance, and Subhashree Bharati for cartographic assistance.

Every effort has been made to acknowledge those individuals, organizations, and corporations that have helped with this book and to trace copyright holders. DK apologizes in advance if any omission has occurred. If an omission does come to light, DK will be pleased to insert the appropriate acknowledgment in the subsequent editions of the book.

The publisher would like to thank the following for their kind permission to reproduce their photographs:

(Key: a-above; b-below/bottom; c-centre; f-far; l-left; r-right; t-top)

6 Dreamstime.com: Mariia Domnikova (bl). **Getty Images:** Moment / Bonnafe Jean-Paul (cl). **7 123RF.com:** andreykuzmin (cr). **Smithsonian Libraries and Archives:** (bc). **8 Library of Congress, Washington, D.C.:** (br). **Wellcome Collection:** An astrologer. Watercolour by an Indian artist, ca. 1825/https://creativecommons.org/publicdomain/mark/1.0 (ca). **9 Dreamstime.com:** Vladimir Lukovic (cl). **© The Metropolitan Museum of Art:** Purchase, John Stewart and Arnold Lieberman, Kurt Berliner, Jonn S. and Jane Wenner, Nancy Wiener Gallery, Helene and Philippe Leloup and Anonymous Gifts, and funds from various donors, 2004 (t). **10-11 Dreamstime.com:** Graphics.vp (cb). **NASA:** (5 (Nova)); GSFC (4). **11 Dreamstime.com:** Claudiodivizia (tr). **12 Alamy Stock Photo:** Dinodia Photos RF (cr). **Dreamstime.com:** Fotoeye75 (bc); Panagiotis Karapanagiotis (cla). **13 Dreamstime.com:** Nicku (clb); Cenk Unver (bc). **14 Dreamstime.com:** Maik Spohn (cla). **NASA:** ESA, J. Hester (Arizona State University) (br). **15 Dreamstime.com:** Chaowarin Hadchiang (cla); Ievgenii Tryfonov (cb). **NASA:** ESA, and J. Lotz and the HFF Team (tr). **16 Dreamstime.com:** Paulpaladin (cla). **Science Photo Library:** Mark Garlick (cb). **17 Dreamstime.com:** Alteraposto (ca); Naresh Sharma (tl); Destina156 (cb). **NASA:** JPL-Caltech / R. Hurt (SSC / Caltech) (bl). **19 NASA:** Johns Hopkins University Applied Physics Laboratory / Southwest Research Institute / Alex Parker (br). **20-21 NASA:** JPL-Caltech, Susan Stolovy (SSC / Caltech) et al. **23 Dorling Kindersley:** NASA (crb). **24 NASA:** (bl). **24-25 Dreamstime.com:** Koolander (c). **25 Dreamstime.com:** Tawatchai Prakobkit (tr). **26-27 NASA:** Goddard / SDO (c). **27 NASA:** Goddard Space Flight Center / Joy Ng (cr). **28-29 NASA:** JPL / USGS (c). **29 NASA:** (br); Caltech-JPL / MIT / SRS (clb). **30 Dreamstime.com:** Vladimir Stanii (b). **31 Dreamstime.com:** Alexstar (cla); Nicoleta Raluca Tudor (crb); Alexander Mirt (br). **32 Dreamstime.com:** Ghadel (ca); Igor Groshev (tr); Sergey Melnikov (clb). **33 Dreamstime.com:** Pressureua (tl); Santos06 (tr); Hongqi Zhang (aka Michael Zhang) (cl). **34 Dreamstime.com:** Lotophagi (crb); Vgorbash (bl). **35 Dreamstime.com:** Matias Del Carmine (cl); Radekgibran (tr/cla); Edgar Parra (bl). **36 Dreamstime.com:** Patrick Guenette (bl); Hsiu Chuan Yu (crb). **37 Dreamstime.com:** Indos82 (cla); Indra Kosasih (tr); Leandroperinpissolato (crb); Relato (bl). **38 The Cleveland Museum Of Art:** Gift of Doris and Ed Wiener 1971.61 (c). **© The Metropolitan Museum of Art:** Gift of Henry G. Marquand, 1897 (br). **39 Dreamstime.com:** Matej Jirka (cl); Yuriykulik (t); Vitalij Kopa (br). **NASA:** Johns Hopkins University Applied Physics Laboratory / Southwest Research Institute (clb). **42 Dreamstime.com:** Photobeard (l); Planetfelicity (c); Tranz2d (cra). **44-45 Dreamstime.com:** Littlepaw (patterns); Valery Nosko. **44 Alamy Stock Photo:** Dinodia Photos RM (br). **45 Dreamstime.com:** Siempreverde22 (cr). **47 Dreamstime.com:** Meinzahn (br). **48 Dreamstime.com:** Jeneses Imre (br); Roomyana (ca). **49 Dreamstime.com:** Patrick Guenette (bl); Channarong Pherngjanda (cr). **50-51 Dreamstime.com:** Andrei Ignatov. **50 Indian Institute of Astrophysics:** (b). **51 Indian Institute of Astrophysics:** Kodaikanal Solar Observatory (cla, cra, br). **NASA:** SDO (tc). **52 Dreamstime.com:** Kevin Carden (crb); Khaneeros Thongboonyang (c, b); Pere Sanz (cr). **52-53 Dreamstime.com:** Khaneeros Thongboonyang. **53 Dreamstime.com:** Borirak Mongkolget (cr); Khaneeros Thongboonyang (t). **54 Dreamstime.com:** Picstudio (bl); Scanrail (br). **University of Calcutta:** (cra). **55 Alamy Stock Photo:** Matteo Omied (cra). **Dreamstime.com:** Sayan Bunard (clb). **56 Alamy Stock Photo:** Keystone Pictures Usa (cl). **56-57 Dreamstime.com:** Fourleaflover. **58 NASA:** ESA / Hubble & NASA (crb); **X-ray:**CXC / Wesleyan Univ. / R.Kilgard, et al; **Optical:**STScI (ca). **58-59 NASA:** European Space Agency (t). **59 NASA:** (crb); ESA / Hubble &amp (cb); ESA, and The Hubble Heritage Team (STScI / AURA) (clb); JPL-Caltech (tc); Goddard Space Flight Center (c); ESA / Hubble (ca). **60 NASA:** JPL-Caltech / University of Wisconsin (tr). **60-61 Dreamstime.com:** Fascinadora. **61 NASA:** JPL-Caltech / University of Wisconsin (tl). **62 Dreamstime.com:** Yap Hong Chan. **62-63 Dreamstime.com:** Ruslangrumble. **63 Dreamstime.com:** Lefteris Papaulakis (br). **64-65 NASA:** ESA / Hubble and the Heritage Team. **66 Alamy Stock Photo:** Dinodia Photos RM (b). **67 Dreamstime.com:** Sergei Nezhinskii (cra). **68 Alamy Stock Photo:** Heritage Image Partnership Ltd / Fine Art Images (bl). **69 Alamy Stock Photo:** Science History Images (bl). **NASA:** (cr). **70-71 Dreamstime.com:** Sirup. **72 Dreamstime.com:** Dragan Ili (bl); Sergei Nezhinskii (bc). **72-73 Indian Space Research Organisation:** Vikram sarabhai sapce centre. **73 Indian Space Research Organisation:** (tl). **74-75 Dreamstime.com:** Valery Nosko. **74 Getty Images:** Pallava Bagla / Corbis Historical (bc). **75 Getty Images:** Pallava Bagla / Corbis News (bl, tr, cra). **Indian Space Research Organisation:** (crb). **78 Alamy Stock Photo:** Dinodia Photos RM (c). **79 Indian Space Research Organisation:** (tl, r). **NASA:** (bl). **80-81 Photo Division, PIB, Ministry of Information and Broadcasting. 81 Indian Space Research Organisation:** (crb). **82-83 Dreamstime.com:** Picstudio (tc). **NASA:** (c). **82 NASA:** (clb); SpaceX (bl); JPL / Ball Aerospace & Technologies Corporation (crb). **83 Dreamstime.com:** Kittipong Jirasukhanont (cra); Yurkoman Yurko (tr); Hrishchenko Oleksandr (bc). **NASA:** (tc). **84-85 Indian Space Research Organisation. 84 Indian Space Research Organisation:** (cl). **85 Indian Space Research Organisation:** (crb, t). **86 123RF.com:** Kittipong Jirasukhanont (clb). **Dreamstime.com:** Igor Sapozhkov (br). **ESA:** CNES / Arianespace / Optique Video du CSG (cra). **87 NASA:** (tl); Lauren Dauphin (cra); Joshua Stevens (ca). **88 Indian Space Research Organisation:** (cl). **88-89 Dreamstime.com:** Andrey Armyagov (b). **89 Indian Space Research Organisation:** (tr). **90 Indian Space Research Organisation:** (br, clb). **91 Indian Space Research Organisation:** (br). **92-93 Getty Images:** UniversalImagesGroup / Planet Observer. **92 Dreamstime.com:** Bob Suir (cra). **93 Dreamstime.com:** Jameschipper (t). **94 Indian Space Research Organisation:** (tc). **96 123RF.com:** rook76 (bl). **Getty Images:** Pallava Bagla / Corbis News (cr). **97-98 Dreamstime.com:** Lavizzara. **97 Getty Images:** Pallava Bagla / Corbis News. **100 Dreamstime.com:** Esquare. Art. Lab. (br); Nlagutkina (cla). **NASA:** (cra). **101 Dreamstime.com:** Tatiana Golmer (br); Pavel Trubnikov (c). **NASA:** (tl). **102 Indian Space Research Organisation:** (cla, cra); Krebs, Gunter D. "Bhaskara 1, 2. Gunter's Space Page. Retrieved January 12, 2022, from https://space.skyrocket.de/doc_sdat/bhaskara-1.htm (br). **102-103 Getty Images:** Jody Amiet / AFP. **103 Indian Space Research Organisation:** (tc, cr). **104 Indian Space Research Organisation:** (cl). **104-105 Indian Space Research Organisation:** (c). **105 Indian Space Research Organisation:** (c, cr). **106 Getty Images:** Hindustan Times / Sunil Saxena (r). **107 Getty Images:** Sondeep Shankar / Hulton Archive (b). **Indian Space Research Organisation:** (r). **108-109 Indian Space Research Organisation:** (t). **112 NASA. 113 NASA. 114 ESA:** BepiColombo / MTM, CC BY-SA 3.0 IGO (br). **NASA:** JPL-Caltech / SwRI / MSSS (cr); JPL / SwRI / MSSS (l). **115 NASA:** (tr, cl); JPL-Caltech (b); Goddard / University of Arizona / Lockheed Martin (tl); ESA, Gerald Cecil (UNC-Chapel Hill) / Image Processing: Joseph DePasquale (STScI) (cr). **116 NASA:** (cla); JPL-Caltech (crb); Dominic Hart (bl). **116-117 Dreamstime.com:** Khaneeros Thongboonyang. **117 Alamy Stock Photo:** NG Images (cl). **NASA:** (tr); Bill Ingalls (br). **118-119 Dreamstime.com:** Beibaoke1 (b); Denis Belitskiy. **119 Indian Institute of Astrophysics:** (tl, tr). **120 Indian Space Research Organisation. 121 Indian Space Research Organisation:** (l, br). **122 Indian Space Research Organisation:** (crb). **NASA:** (bl); ESA / SOHO (cla). **123 ESA:** (ca). **NASA:** (br, bc); McREL (tl); PL-Caltech (tr); JPL-Caltech (c). **124 Indian Space Research Organisation:** (b). **124-125 Indian Space Research Organisation:** (t). **126 Getty Images:** Stocktrek RF (clb). **127 NASA:** JPL-Caltech / University of Arizona (tr); JPL-Caltech / MSSS (c). **128 Indian Space Research Organisation:** (crb). **128-129 Indian Space Research Organisation:** (c). **129 Indian Space Research Organisation:** (t, clb). **130 Getty Images:** Pallava Bagla / Corbis News (cl). **131 Getty Images:** Pallava Bagla / Corbis News (cla). **Indian Space Research Organisation:** (tr). **132-133 IUCAA. 134 Indian Space Research Organisation:** (b). **135 Indian Space Research Organisation:** (t). **NASA:** (br). **136 Dreamstime.com:** Pixeldigital (bl). **ESA:** DLR / FU Berlin (G. Neukum), CC BY-SA 3.0 IGO (cl). **137 Dreamstime.com:** Beholdereye. **NASA:** ESO / M. Kornmesser (c); Goddard Space Flight Center / CI Lab (bl). **138 NASA:** JPL-Caltech. **139 Depositphotos Inc:** everett225 (cl). **Dreamstime.com:** Georgios Kollidas (tl). **ESO:** EHT Collaboration (bl). **Getty Images:** Bettmann (cra). **IUCAA:** (crb). **140-141 Dreamstime.com:** Roman Egorov; Ahmad Safarudin (b). **141 Getty Images:** Patrick T. Fallon / AFP (tr). **142 Photo Division, PIB, Ministry of Information and Broadcasting. 142-143 Dreamstime.com:** Mitsibart. **143 Indian PostsTelegraph Department, GOI:** (b). **144-145 Getty Images:** Pallava Bagla / Corbis News. **146-147 Dreamstime.com:** Shmel. **147 NASA:** Desiree Stover (br)

All other images © Dorling Kindersley